DESIGNING FOR THE WEB

Getting Started in a New Medium

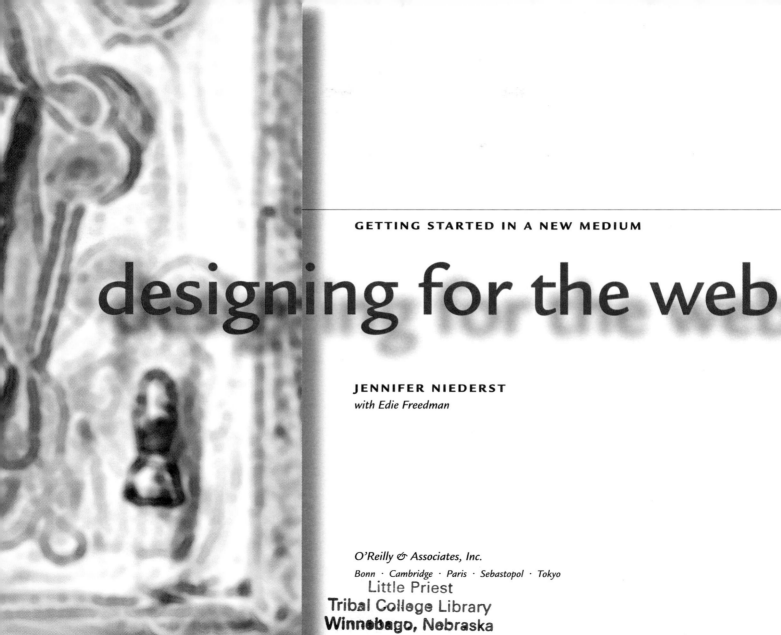

GETTING STARTED IN A NEW MEDIUM

designing for the web

JENNIFER NIEDERST

with Edie Freedman

O'Reilly & Associates, Inc.

Bonn · Cambridge · Paris · Sebastopol · Tokyo

Designing for the Web: Getting Started in a New Medium

by Jennifer Niederst, with Edie Freedman

Editor: Linda Mui
Production Editor: Nicole Gipson Arigo

Printing History:
  April 1996: First Edition

ISBN: 1-56592-165-8

contents

foreword

N THE EARLY DAYS OF O'REILLY & ASSOCIATES, we didn't have any design-ers, just writers. For us, a well-designed manual was produced from a logical outline organized according to what was most important to the user. A manual was mostly text.

When we started publishing our own books, we enlisted the services of book design-ers, who paid attention to how text was displayed on the page. I wasn't thinking of it at the time, but in many ways a book designer creates a user interface for the text.

When we began experimenting with the World Wide Web early in 1993, I realized online communications was on the verge of becoming a visual medium. Instead of text scrolling on an ASCII terminal screen, users would interact with linked pages consist-ing of styled text and graphics. I needed a designer for this Web experiment, and Jen-nifer Niederst, one of O'Reilly's book designers, was willing to work hard at creating a user interface for online text.

I gave this Web site experiment its name, *Global Network Navigator* (GNN), and it became the first commercial Web site. Jennifer Niederst gave GNN its "look-and-feel."

First, Jennifer came up with a delightful hot-air balloon as a logo image that cap-tured the spirit of GNN and gave it a face people would recognize. Then she developed the basic navigational mechanisms for the site and mastheads or banners for each of the major areas. She worked hard to learn—and work around—the constraints of the medium. At times, it was frustrating for her because she could not control everything as she did when she designed for print.

In the end, Jennifer created the colorful shape of the users' experiences. It was what stuck in their minds when they visited and recalled when they came back time and again. Moreover, Jennifer worked to redesign the site several times based on new ideas for how to improve the user experience.

Throughout this time, Jennifer worked extensively with O'Reilly's creative director, Edie Freedman, who has also contributed to this book. Edie is a versatile designer who gave O'Reilly books their public face, a collection of distinctive animal covers. Edie established the direction for O'Reilly design work: classic yet unexpected and fresh, aiming at improving rather than interfering with communication.

There are plenty of Web sites today, and there are lots of graphical pages, but there is not yet much evidence that many designers are at work on the Web. This book hopes to remedy that problem. Jennifer could have chosen to write a book with the intention of making everyday users better designers. Instead, Jennifer has written a book for designers that will help them bring their expertise to the Web. What she asks of the designer-coming-to-the-Web is a willingness to study techniques that have at most several years of practice.

After GNN was sold to America Online in June of 1995, Jennifer became creative director at Songline Studios, a company I created with backing from AOL and O'Reilly & Associates to develop original online content. Our first product at Songline was an online magazine named *Web Review.* Jennifer certainly made use of her experience at GNN in designing *Web Review,* but she also had to disregard her previous experience at times. She had to question whether many assumptions we made in the design of GNN were still true. The pace of the Internet challenges you to apply what you learn and to unlearn what no longer seems to apply. Therefore, designing Web sites is largely about redesigning Web sites. The work never seems to end.

In the end, Jennifer has done terrific work on the Web, and this book will help you learn from her experience, which is as great as anyone's in this new medium. Certainly anyone interested in the Web can learn and benefit from the techniques Jennifer explains in this book. Yet the trained designer will benefit the most, and put these techniques to the best use by supplying his or her own creative vision. This attention to design will only make the Web a better experience for all users, and help establish the level of professionalism that the Web needs to become a credible communications medium.

Dale Dougherty

President & CEO, Songline Studios
Sebastopol, California

preface   a few words before we begin

Y MOTHER RECENTLY MET A YOUNG WOMAN who said she was a designer. Being one of these people who starts up conversations with strangers, my mother told the woman that her daughter was a designer on the Web. The stranger looked up with surprise and newfound respect, and said, "You're kidding! Everyone wants to get into that! She must be cutting edge!"

Well, I don't know about being cutting edge, but it does seem like a lot of designers want to know more about the World Wide Web, or they *need* to know more as a result of a growing demand for Web pages by their clients. The Web has been described many different ways, surrounded by buzzwords and acronyms and elaborate diagrams, but essentially it's just a new medium.

Granted, it's a revolutionary new medium, but since it is still visual, designers are needed for all the same reasons they've been needed before:

- to organize information for the most effective communication

- to guide readers' eyes through the information

- to make the document distinct and eye-catching

This book won't teach you how to design, but it does aim to give you the information you need to adapt your skills to the Web.

I've been designing Web documents for nearly three years now—that's almost as long as the Web as we know it today has been around! By necessity, I was self-taught and relied on my co-workers for feedback, technical information, and support.

Accumulating the basic facts and special tricks I have under my belt today was a slow, gradual process. I wished at the time that there was just one place I could go to quickly learn all the technical stuff, without having to ferret it out myself, so I could get on to doing what I enjoyed the most—*designing!*

The Web provides possibilities, limitations, and challenges that have required me to develop a specialized way of thinking when I'm designing for it. Although there's no substitute for learning through experimentation and experience, I'd like to give you a short-cut to the basic information you need so you can quickly get to the business of designing. My goal is to save you some time.

■ THE DESIGNER'S ROLE

When people say they are "Web page designers," they can mean a lot of things. I usually tell designers who are interested in the Web that they can be as "geeky as they wanna be."

In print design, a number of tasks contribute to a final product, such as providing illustrations, specifying type, laying out the document, adjusting the trapping in pre-press, and running the 4-color press. The same applies to creating a Web site. A Web page designer might be responsible for the following tasks:

- providing the graphics only in the form of individual files

- learning enough coding language to create samples, then relying on a production department to create the final, technically correct files that go online

- providing complete, functional Web site packages

- developing and maintaining scripts for Web forms and automatic document generation (known as CGI scripting)

- maintaining and configuring the server software

So the role of the designer can range from just "drawing the pictures" to becoming a complete Web geek.

This book assumes that you are more interested in designing than programming. I'll concentrate on teaching you what you need to know to create graphics that are especially tailored for the Web, and enough about Web documents that you'll feel comfortable creating basic Web pages and linking them together to form a site. I'd like to lay a foundation to get you up and running.

■ HOW THIS BOOK IS ORGANIZED

Sifting through all the Web design facts floating around in my head and piecing them together in a clear and meaningful way has perhaps been the largest challenge in creating this book. The topic is rife with chicken-and-egg scenarios and intertwined elements. In the end, three major topics have emerged.

Part I: The new environment

The Web is like no other medium. This section describes the landscape of the Web, introduces you to a host of new terms and concepts, and illuminates some peculiarities you can expect to encounter. I begin with some general information on how it all works, and then cut right to the chase and demonstrate how a Web page is put together.

Part II: All about graphics for the Web

As the title advertises, this part deals strictly with Web graphics: the basic specifications, how to create them, and how to fine-tune them. There are also chapters on Web-specific graphics effects such as transparency, interlacing, and imagemaps.

Part III: About the rest of the page

Obviously, creating the graphics is only part of Web page design. Even if you are not ultimately responsible for creating the final files, it's essential that you have a basic understanding of what can and can't be done online. Again, aimed more at design than programming, this section provides a sampling of tags I use most often to "design" a page as well as an introduction to some of the other elements that can be added to a Web page. I'll also take a brief look at multi-page documents and some basic interface issues.

■ MAC-CENTRICITY

The vast majority of design professionals I know are loyal Mac users. Despite the recent availability of graphics applications for Windows and PCs with the power to drive them, the Mac remains the darling of the design world. For that reason, I've chosen to keep this book fairly Mac-centric.

Since the Web isn't platform-specific, this orientation won't make any difference to the majority of the discussions and explanations at hand. It does, however, come into play in the tutorials, which feature the Macintosh interface and Mac-based tools. Browsers and commercial applications such as Adobe Photoshop are available for both the Mac and Windows platforms, and work just about the same. In the cases of certain shareware demonstrations, which *are* only available on the Mac, I've done my best to at least point out the Windows equivalents with information on where to get them.

■ ACKNOWLEDGMENTS

This book came perilously close to not happening at all, so I'd like to thank those people who had something to do with the fact that it did. Thanks go to Edie Freedman, who brought me on this book-writing roller-coaster ride in the first place. She and Linda Mui, editor extraordinaire, shared that first car with me as we careened over the peaks and valleys. Thank you to Frank Willison and Kerri Bonasch, whose words of encouragement prevented me from chickening out while still in line. In the end, it's been a great ride!

Thanks to all those who have contributed hands-on time to the project: David Freedman, Marcia Ciro, Kerrie Kennedy, and Daniel Austin for their insightful comments; the production gang at O'Reilly & Associates, Inc.—Chris Reilley, Sheryl Avruch, Nicole Gipson Arigo, Clairemarie Fisher O'Leary, and Sue Willing—for accepting a new challenge and minding the details; and to Seventeenth Street Studios for their creativity and hard work.

Thanks to Jeff Robbins, for all he's taught me, and to all the other people who have shared their knowledge, including John Labovitz, Tim Stevenson, my buddies on the GNN team, and my friends at Songline Studios. My gratitude goes especially to Dale Dougherty for creating tremendous opportunities for me in this new frontier.

Finally, I'd like to thank my Mom and Dad for a great set of genes and the support and guidance to put them to good use, and to my brother, Liam, for endless inspiration. My heartfelt thanks go to Chris Geary, whose patience with me has been heroic.

the new environment

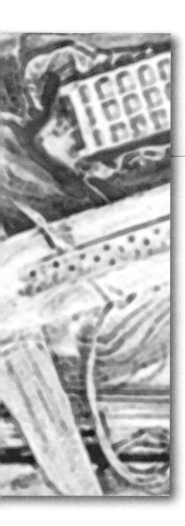

one   how the web works

HE FIRST TIME I SAW A WEB PAGE, I wasn't quite sure what I was looking at. On the monitor appeared what looked like a word processing application with a simple document in the window. Click on the blue word, and *presto*, a new document popped into view! Although I don't wish to rob you of the magic (there's still plenty that's magical about the Web), it's important to look behind the scenes at how those documents end up on your screen. You'll also need to familiarize yourself with some of the terminology (and acronyms, acronyms, acronyms) you'll hear in this new arena. I promise to keep this as brief and simple as possible.

■ THE ANATOMY OF A WEB PAGE

You may be as surprised as I was to learn that the graphically rich, interactive pages are generated by simple, text-only documents. That's right: plain old ASCII files. It seemed to me that there must be something more to it than that.

HTML documents

The "magic" in these files is that they contain special tags that explain how the text is to be displayed, where graphics should go, and where links occur. This system of tagging is called *HyperText Markup Language*, or HTML for short, and the tags are commonly known as HTML tags. "Hypertext" means that a document contains links to other documents. It's all the linking between documents that led this part of the Internet to be called the "Web."

Let's take a look at a very simple HTML document (Figure 1-1).

FIGURE 1-1 ▶
Simple HTML document

```
<HTML>
<HEAD>
<TITLE>Jen's Fake Home Page</TITLE>
</HEAD>
<BODY>
<IMG SRC="star.gif"><IMG SRC="jenbanner.gif"><IMG SRC="star.gif">
<CENTER><H1>Welcome to my Web Page</H1></CENTER>
<IMG SRC="exclamation.gif" ALIGN=left HSPACE=6>
<STRONG>Warning!</STRONG>This is not my <EM>real</EM> home
page. It's just a little something I made up for the occasion. But just in
case you're interested, I'll tell you a bit about me.
<HR>
<H2>Places I've Lived</H2>
<UL>
<LI>Akron, OH
<LI>Hudson, OH
<LI>South Bend, IN
<LI>Boston, MA
</UL>
</BODY>
</HTML>
```

■ TIP:

You can see the HTML file for any page on the Web by choosing "View Source" or "View Document by Source" in your browser's menu. It's a good way to peek at the tagging that is responsible for an effect you like. Your browser will open the source document in a separate window.

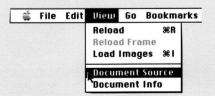

What have we here?

The tags are made up of an open bracket (or less-than sign), <, a string of characters that describes the tag's action, and a closing bracket (or greater-than sign), >. Anything between brackets is hidden when the file is displayed.

Most tags contain information that affects how text is handled. For example, the <H1> tag means the following text as a first-level heading, the <LI> tag says that the following text is a list item, and so on.

Most tags appear in pairs (sometimes called containers), the first one turning that attribute "on" and the second one turning it "off." In the example above, <EM> indicates that the following text should be emphasized; </EM> ends the emphasized text and switches back to normal text.

Before HTML there was **SGML** (**Standard Generalized Markup Language**), which established the system of describing documents in terms of structure, independent of appearance. SGML tags work the same way as the HTML tags we've seen, but there are far more of them, enabling a more sophisticated description of document elements.

Publishers have begun storing SGML versions of their documents so that they can be translated into a variety of end uses. The tags may be rendered one way if the end product is a printed book and another way for a CD-ROM. The advantage is that a single source file can be used to create a variety of end products.

HTML is similar but is tailored for online functions, such as links to other documents. The principle of logical tagging is the same.

* There are a few browser-specific tags that do contain limited style information such as changing the font size or changing colors. Although useful, these tags are contrary to the concept of HTML as a universal language.

There are also tags that add elements to the page. In Figure 1-1, <IMG...> means "put a graphic here" and <HR> says "draw a horizontal rule."

Logical by nature

I don't want to bog you down with too much HTML at this point, but for now, you should note that tags that affect text describe the *type* of information that follows. It's similar to the categories you'd create in a style sheet in a word processing or desktop publishing application.

It's also very important to note that the tags do not contain specific style information such as what font to use, what font size to display, and how much space goes above and below the text.* And guess what: *you don't get to specify these things!* They are determined by the software that displays the document and the person using that software. It's like setting up all the categories in your style sheet, but not being able to fill in the specs for each one. It was rather shocking for me at first. Suddenly, all the things I was responsible for controlling were out of my control. The small consolation was that I *could* control the appearance of anything I put in a graphic.

But where are the pictures?

One look at the Web will tell you that there's more to it than just text. In fact, it has been the ability to display graphics on the screen that has led to the Web's mass appeal. But if the graphics don't appear in the HTML file, where are they?

Each graphic on a Web page is actually an individual graphic file that exists separately from the HTML document (Figure 1-2). It is brought into the page by the <IMG> tag (mentioned above) when the document is displayed on your screen.

Easy as pie!

For the most part, HTML tagging is a simple affair. There are only about a dozen core tags that will cover most of what you'll need to do, and it's not difficult to learn to use them. And since the finished product is just a text file, you can use any basic text editor that can save ASCII text, such as SimpleText or Microsoft Word (although specialized tools are available to automate the process somewhat).

FIGURE 1-2 ▶
The text and the graphics are separate pieces

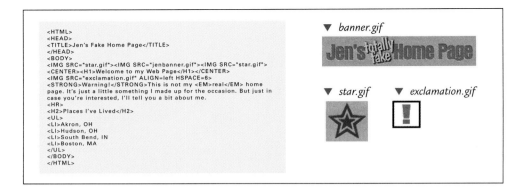

```
<HTML>
<HEAD>
<TITLE>Jen's Fake Home Page</TITLE>
</HEAD>
<BODY>
<IMG SRC="star.gif"><IMG SRC="jenbanner.gif"><IMG SRC="star.gif">
<CENTER><H1>Welcome to my Web Page</H1></CENTER>
<IMG SRC="exclamation.gif" ALIGN=left HSPACE=6>
<STRONG>Warning!</STRONG>This is not my <EM>real</EM> home
page. It's just a little something I made up for the occasion. But just in
case you're interested, I'll tell you a bit about me.
<HR>
<H2>Places I've Lived</H2>
<UL>
<LI>Akron, OH
<LI>Hudson, OH
<LI>South Bend, IN
<LI>Boston, MA
</UL>
</BODY>
</HTML>
```

▼ *banner.gif*

▼ *star.gif*   ▼ *exclamation.gif*

Of course, some HTML documents can get to be quite complicated, but regardless of number and features of the tags, it's all based on the simple concept of using tags to describe elements in the document. Chapter 11, *A designer's guide to HTML*, contains more detailed information about specific tags and what they do.

■ BROWSERS

A *browser* is a piece of software you run on your computer that displays HTML documents and graphics. If the Internet were a television broadcasting network, the browser would be the television set you need to see the shows.

For example, Figure 1-3 shows one way our sample HTML file might look when viewed through a browser.

The browser reads through the HTML file (also called the *source* file) and renders the text between tags as it comes to them. Receiving instructions sequentially from a string of characters in a file is what makes HTML tagging resemble a programming language. Like most designers, I've been fortunate to be spared direct contact with the code that builds my designs. So when I first started using HTML it helped me to picture the tags and text in the source file as "beads on a string" that the browser deals with one by one.

FIGURE 1-3 ▶

Sample HTML file from Figure 1-1.
The browser brings the separate text
and graphic files together.

```
<HTML>
<HEAD>
<TITLE>Jen's Fake Home Page</TITLE>
</HEAD>
<BODY>
<IMG SRC="star.gif"><IMG SRC="jenbanner.gif"><IMG SRC="star.gif">
<CENTER><H1>Welcome to my Web Page</H1></CENTER>
<IMG SRC="exclamation.gif" ALIGN=left HSPACE=6>
<STRONG>Warning!</STRONG>This is not my <EM>real</EM> home
page. It's just a little something I made up for the occasion. But just in
case you're interested, I'll tell you a bit about me.
<HR>
<H2>Places I've Lived</H2>
<UL>
<LI>Akron, OH
<LI>Hudson, OH
<LI>South Bend, IN
<LI>Boston, MA
</UL>
</BODY>
</HTML>
```

In the text of our sample HTML file, the browser first encounters the `<HTML>` tag, which says what follows is an HTML file. Next, a `<BODY>` tag tells it that what follows is the body of that file that should be displayed in the browser's window. Then it hits a tag, `<IMG SRC="banner.gif">`, that tells it to look for a graphic called "banner.gif" and display it. When it reads the `<H1>` tag, it knows to start displaying the following text as a large header, until the "end header" tag, `</H1>`, tells it to stop. And so on throughout the document until it gets to the end.

In fact, browsers are more or less one-trick ponies—they access HTML documents and render the information between the tags in a way that differentiates the various types of information.

Because the browser is so fundamental to how Web pages appear to the end user, designers need to be especially aware of some of the complex issues surrounding browser software. For this reason, after this brief introduction, I have dedicated an entire chapter to some of the ins and outs of dealing with browsers (Chapter 2, *More about browsers*).

What you can't do with a browser

Knowing what a browser doesn't do is as important as knowing what it does. Simply put, a Web browser is *not* a tool for creating Web pages. (There are other tools for doing that which we will be getting to later.)

In addition, you can't use a browser to edit a Web page you see in the window. When you access a Web page, you are actually just given a view of it, not access to the file itself. You can't edit that file, in the same way that you can't use your television to affect the outcome of a TV show. The only way to change a document is to replace the document on the computer that is storing it.

It is tempting at first, after spending so much time in WYSIWYG document layout programs, to want to click on an image and drag it into a new position or to change a little text right there in the window. But you can't because a browser is designed only to *view* the documents.

■ THE "CLIENT-SERVER" MODEL

This is one of those terms that might send laypeople running. All "client-server" really means is that the information lives on one machine on the network and sends it to other machines upon request.

The machine that stores and serves the Web documents is called the server, and the program that you use to request and view these documents is called the client. On the Web, the browser is the client.

When people refer to "client-side" applications, they mean that the applications are running on the user's machine, not the server.

■ SERVERS

So, those HTML documents have to reside somewhere, right? They aren't all sitting in one place, but are literally scattered all over the globe.

The World Wide Web is a network of sites on the Internet that provide information and services. That sounds rather lofty, but picture very ordinary-looking computers, ranging from high-powered UNIX mainframes to ordinary personal computers (both PCs and Macs), in offices around the world. But there are a couple of things that make these computers special. First, they are connected to the Internet, and second, and most importantly, they are running programs that make certain documents on them accessible to millions of users.

The programs that make documents accessible are called *servers*. It's also common to call computers that run server software "servers" as well.

Each server has a unique *host name*, such as *jasper.ora.com*. The host name is needed to identify the server on the Internet, so your browser can connect to the right machine. On the Web, it's a convention that machines running Web servers often have a host name starting with "www" (such as *www.ora.com*), but this is by no means a hard-and-fast rule.

■ FINDING A WEB PAGE

With all those Web pages on all those servers, how would you ever find the one you're looking for? Fortunately, each document has its own special address called a URL (Uniform Resource Locator). If you can only learn one Web acronym today, it should be this one. It is a way of saying "Web address," but "U-R-L" is the preferred lingo. To view a specific Web page, type its URL into your browser, and *voila!*

Even if you've never actually used the World Wide Web, it's getting so you can't get through a day without seeing a crazy-looking string of characters beginning with "http://," whether on the side of a bus, at the end of a television commercial, or in the credits of a movie. It may look confusing, but each part tells the browser what it needs to know to access the page. The following diagram shows the most common components of a URL.

Often, you will see URLs that stop after the host name and do not contain the name of a specific file. This is possible due to a built-in default in the server software.

If the browser doesn't ask for a specific file name in a directory, the server searches for a file named index.html in that directory, and if found, the browser displays that file. By naming your top-level document (most likely your home page) index.html, you can keep your URL more simple.

Therefore, when you enter the URL *http://gnn.com/wr/*, the browser is actually displaying *http://gnn.com/wr/index.html*.

Note that if the wr directory hadn't contained a file named index.html, the simplified URL would cause the browser to display the entire contents of that directory in the window. Naming a file index.html also has the advantage of preventing the world from being able to snoop around in your server directories.

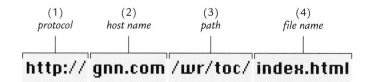

As shown above, a URL is made up of the following bits of information:

(1) indicates what "protocol" to use. For most Web documents, the protocol is HTTP (Hypertext Transfer Protocol). That is why Web servers are also sometimes called HTTP servers.

(2) indicates which server to connect to. The URL identifies a server by its host name.

(3) indicates the path to the file or the hierarchical directories the browser needs to go through to get to the file. If you are most familiar with the Macintosh, you're probably accustomed to organizing your files in hierarchical folders. It's a good idea to adjust slightly and think in terms of directories, as I will throughout this book.

(4) the name of the file to access. In our example, the file name is *index.html*.

So what our example says is that you want to use the HTTP protocol to connect to the host on the Internet called *gnn.com* and request the document */wr/toc/index.html*.

It's important to be familiar with basic URL structure when you are building links into your documents. I will discuss links further in Chapter 4, *Creating hypertext links*.

■ **PUTTING IT ALL TOGETHER**

Let's take a look at the stream of events that occur with every Web page that appears on your screen (Figure 1-4).

You request a Web page either by clicking on text that is linked to that page or by typing its URL (address) directly into the browser using the "Open Location" menu item. Among other things, the URL names what host to connect to and what file to request on that host.

FIGURE 1-4 ▶

Behind the scenes on the Web

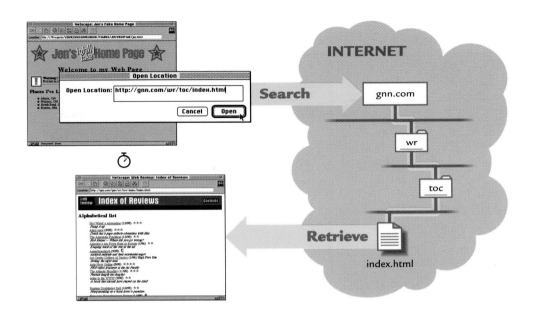

The browser contacts the Web server on the host named in the URL, requesting the file. The Web server searches for the file requested, and either returns it to the browser or returns an error that it can't be accessed. Assuming the file is found and is sent across the network successfully, the browser displays the document according to the formatting specified in the document's HTML tags.

If the file contains inline graphics, the browser contacts the server again for each graphic. Each graphic is sent individually. As they arrive, the browser then inserts the graphics into the HTML document where specified.

■ HOW DO I GET MY PAGE ON THE WEB?

Creating a Web page design is not enough. Your document(s) need to be stored on a server in order to be accessible to all Internet users. By putting your files on the server, you are officially publishing your pages.

Chances are that the machine you use to create graphics and HTML files is not running the software necessary to make it a server. Therefore, you'll need to get access to space on a computer that is configured for the job.

If you are on your own, you can find a local Internet Service Provider (that's ISP, in the biz) that offers space on a Web server to their customers. It is typical to receive anywhere from five to twenty MB of storage on a machine to do with as you please.

One place to start looking is the Yahoo directory *(http://www.yahoo.com)* under Business and Economy/Companies/ Internet Service Providers. Online services such as GNN and Prodigy also provide space on their server for subscribers' Web pages.

If you are designing a Web page for somebody else, it's likely that person (or company) has assumed the responsibility of obtaining space on a server for the site.

In either case, be sure to establish communication early on with the server administrator or someone who is familiar with the machine and the process for transferring files onto it. It's similar to learning to work with a new service bureau.

There are some basic questions you should ask early on, such as:

- What kind of computer is it? If it is a PC , are there restrictions on how files are named, such as limiting the name to eight characters with a three character suffix?

- Should your files be organized in any particular way?

- How much traffic (simultaneous requests from browsers) can it handle? Does that number match up with your expectations for your site?

- How would they prefer to receive the files? On floppy disk or some other storage device? Transferred directly over the Internet? This may require learning a little more about UNIX and how the Internet works. I use a Macintosh utility called Fetch for moving files from my Mac to our UNIX server. Fetch provides a simple Mac interface to the clunky business of FTP (file transfer protocol, a method for moving/copying files from one computer to another on the Internet). You can download a copy of Fetch directly from the Internet at this URL: *http://www.dartmouth.edu/pages/softdev/fetch.html.*

- Is the server configured to handle imagemapped graphics (graphics with more than one "hotspot"; for more information, see chapter 10)? Is it configured to handle any other advanced Web functions such as RealAudio or server push? (For more information on these technologies, see Chapter 12, *More Web tricks*.)

two   more about browsers

BECAUSE IT IS THE BROWSER that is ultimately responsible for how a Web page will look to a user, it is essential that designers become familiar with the browser's function and possibilities, as well as its limitations. It is the unpredictable nature of designing pages that may be viewed through a variety of browsers, rather than fixed on paper, slide, or CD-ROM, that makes Web design different from designing for any other medium.

An HTML file contains all the information needed for the construction of a Web page, but it is the browser's job to put it all together visually. One of the first things to get used to as a Web designer is that you have no way of knowing exactly how your page is going to look to the user.

As we've seen in the brief description of HTML in Chapter 1, *How the Web works*, HTML tags contain only generic labels for describing types of information. They don't allow for font or size specifications, or any of the things that designers are accustomed to choosing.* When a browser encounters each tag, it uses either its own built-in defaults or the user's chosen settings to display the information.

The fact that there are dozens of competing browsers available across three major platforms (Macintosh, PC, and UNIX) in the hands of millions of individual users means that there are potentially endless variations of how your carefully crafted Web page will appear in the end. At times, it's maddening.

*Well, OK, there are a few tags out there that affect fonts and sizes, but they aren't part of the HTML standard and only work with specific browsers. For simplicity's sake, I think it's best to overlook these tags for now.

Browsers are programmed with default settings for the display of text and backgrounds, but they also allow individual users to create their own settings for how they'd like to view information on their screens. If you look in the "preferences" settings for any browser, you will find controls for setting some basic attributes such as font, text size, and background color. In fact, giving the end user the final control over appearance is fundamental to the HTML concept.

Text and background

Let's take a look at our sample document viewed on the same browser, but by two users with radically different taste (Figure 2-1). The person on the left is viewing Web pages with pretty standard "out of the can" browser settings of small black text on a light background. However, the user on the right prefers to see all Web pages with large, lime-green sans serif type on a lovely purple background. Granted, this example

▼ FIGURE 2-1
Same HTML document as seen by two different users

may seem extreme, but it's risky to make any assumptions about how your audience prefers to read on-screen.

I remember receiving a particularly enlightening bit of email from a disgruntled reader. It seems he couldn't see my graphics with his preferred browser settings of a dark gray background with white text, so he demanded that I stop making graphics that contained black text and line drawings. I didn't change my graphics, but I did thank him for challenging my assumptions that all people will choose to view dark text on a light background. See, you just never know.

In addition to color preferences, I have seen many surfers set the text size REALLY LARGE to make on-screen reading less stressful for the eyes. So, although you'd like five lines of text to stack next to your logo graphic as it appears on your browser, you can't be sure that what *you* see is what *they'll* get.

Window size

Another user-variable is the size of the browser window. Since users can resize their browser window to fit their monitor, or just to suit their tastes, it is impossible to know just how much of your design they will see at once or how it will appear. This makes fastidious efforts at getting text and graphics to align "just so" just a waste of time (Figure 2-2).

FIGURE 2-2 ▶
Same HTML document as seen on different window sizes

One solution to this problem is to tell users how you'd like them to size the screen. Every now and then, you'll run into a friendly note at the top of a Web page that says, "For optimal viewing of this site, please size your browser this wide" followed by a graphical bar of a certain width. The best you can do is hope that users will play along.

Graphics

Not only can you not be sure of how your graphics will align on the reader's page, you can't even be sure they'll be seeing them at all. Here's a sad fact for designers: users can opt to just turn your graphics off completely! In that case they'll see a generic graphic icon in its place. (See Figure 2-3.) All your hard work for nothing! You can hardly blame them, actually, particularly folks perusing the Web from home with 14.4 Kbs or slower modems. For them, downloading even a simple graphic can take a long time, and usually time equals money paid for online access. We will discuss the ramifications of download times in more depth in the graphics portion of this book, but for now, just know that the graphics you create may never be seen by some viewers.

So now that we've seen how any individual user has the power to completely screw up your beautiful design (just kidding), just wait 'til we talk about what happens when it hits different browsers.

FIGURE 2-3 ▶
Sample document viewed on graphical browser with graphics turned off

▪ THE SAME DOCUMENT CAN LOOK DIFFERENT FROM BROWSER TO BROWSER

When I first started designing for the Web (here's where I get to talk like an old-timer and after only three years in the field!), there was only one graphical browser, NCSA Mosaic, which ran on the UNIX platform. Its functionality was incredibly limited compared to all the features of browsers currently on the market, but in some ways, I still sort of long for those simpler times.

Now there are dozens of browsers on the market and four or five "biggies"* that are wrestling for control of the market. For Web designers (at least for me), this means keeping a finger on the emerging (and vanishing) browsers and the features they offer.

As I discussed earlier, browsers do come hardwired with their own ways of rendering HTML tags. For example, I used the <H1> tag to tell the browser that I'd like the text "Welcome to my home page" to be a first-level heading. However, once again, it is up to the browser to determine how a first-level heading will look. One browser renders it in 18-point Times bold by default, but another browser may make it 24-point Helvetica bold.

Let's take a look at our sample home page as it might appear on several browsers (Figure 2-4).

Needless to say, this is just a small sampling. We could fill volumes with screen shots of how every browser running on every platform would render a sample document. The simple point to be taken from this figure, as I mentioned before, is that a Web page's appearance can be dramatically different on different browsers.**

One reason for the difference is superficial. It has to do with how the browsers are configured to display text. In the first example, the browser uses Times for the text and gray for the background. In the second example, the browser chooses Helvetica and white. As we've seen, users can change these attributes to their preferences anyway.

The other reason is more fundamental, as it has to do with functionality. Browsers are not created equal. Some can do fancy tricks, some perform as reliable workhorses, and others offer just bare-bones access to information. The browser in the third example in Figure 2-4 is an example of the low end of this scale. It is a text-only browser called Lynx, and although it may look ancient, it is still used by people who are

FIGURE 2-4 ▶
Same page on a variety of browsers

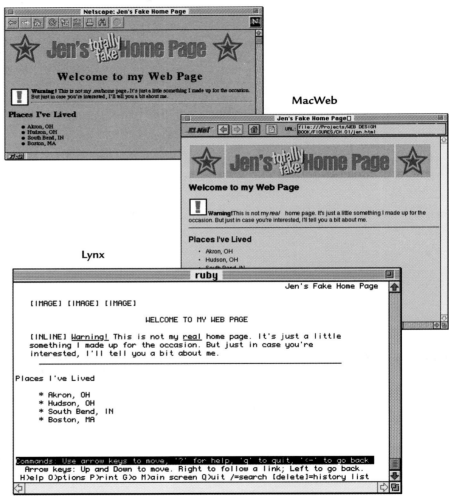

accessing the Internet through simple terminal connections.* Again, here's another section of the Web-browsing audience who won't see your graphics at all because their browser doesn't support graphics.

This brings me to HTML standards. Sounds kinda dry and technical. Well, it is, but it's also really important for designers to know about, since aside from the graphics you create, HTML tags are your tools for this medium.

■ HTML 2.0 AND "EXTENSIONS"

In the old days (there I go again!), there was one set of tags and it worked with all the existing browsers. A certain browser might render the text in the tag according to different stylistic specifications, but at least it was programmed with instructions on what to do when it encountered that tag.

Now, things have changed, and there are basically two types of tags: those that work on every browser, and those that only work on some of them. Allow me to explain this in more depth.

Tags for all browsers

Most technology that is developed over the Internet begins as a proposal, followed by some discussion and fine-tuning. Finally, it is adopted as the standard, and the Internet community cooperates by using that standard. Usually, end users never need to know the details of the process; they just get a finished product. It's sort of like how a bill gets mangled in Congress into a law—in the end, the only thing that affects citizens is the final version of the law.

The system for tagging HTML documents went through this process, and the version that is accepted as the current standard is known as HTML 2.0.** Since it is the standard, you will find that all current browsers will know how to interpret these tags, so you can use them with confidence that they won't be ignored.

In addition, all tools that are being developed for creating Web documents (HTML editors, drag-n-drop page developers, etc.) are sure to have tools and short-cuts built in for using these tags.

*By a simple terminal connection, I mean one in which all you see is text, usually 80 characters by 24 lines. All commands have to be typed, and there are no pull-down menus or clickable buttons.

**Actually, HTML 2.0 is only the *accepted* standard. As of this writing, it hasn't actually gotten its official seal of approval. At the same time, work is being done on developing HTML 3.0, but the process is slow, and the community isn't waiting for it.

Enter Netscape

As you will come to find, the standard set of tags is extremely limited when it comes to page presentation. As more publishers and businesses (not to mention *designers*) came onto the Web, there was more demand for greater control over how their information looked. Although the newer version of HTML (version 3.0) addressed many of their needs, the new spec was mired down in the standard-approval process (still is, as of this printing).

One company, Netscape Communications, founded by the creators of the original NCSA Mosaic, decided not to wait. They were developing a commercial browser with the mission of fixing the things that Mosaic did wrong, as well as adding a number of advanced features that eventually made the Netscape browser by far the most widely used browser on the Web.

As part of this redesign process, they also created a whole slew of special tags, now known as "Netscape extensions" to HTML, which did just the kind of things designers were dying for. Suddenly Web page creators could center text (seems basic, but HTML 2.0 can't do that), wrap text around graphics (again, a pretty simple request), or specify the background color instead of leaving it to fate.

The thing is, those tags only worked with their Netscape browser; thus, the controversy. Because they jumped the gun and bypassed the standards committee, and because these were proprietary tags that only worked on their browser, much of the Web community was up in arms at their debut. To make matters worse, some of the tags specified *style* information right in the HTML file, flying in the face of the HTML ideals of a strictly logical description of elements in a document and of giving control of presentation to the end user. The purists shrieked or shuddered. Others cheered the new possibilities the tags offered and jumped right in.

The debate is waning, but it's an important part of Web history.

Should you use extensions?

Well, I do. There are so many irresistible features—wrapping text around graphics is my favorite example—that it's difficult not to. Web designers quickly discovered that they could create more sophisticated-looking sites, and the Netscape extensions exploded into widespread use.

Many designers who use them liberally find security in the fact that the vast majority of Web users *are* using Netscape, and, not surprisingly, other browsers are gradually supporting some of these Netscape extensions in their new releases. Soon, I expect the current set of extensions will become a *de facto* standard. No doubt by that time, there will be some other proprietary features to worry about.

If the Netscape extensions weren't bad enough, now Microsoft has hit the scene with its own proprietary tags that only work with their Internet Explorer browser. It's unlikely that this standards war will ever settle down since it is in the interest of companies like Netscape and Microsoft to offer features that might give their technology an edge, keeping them one step ahead. This competition in itself contradicts the whole standards idea.

The thing to know is that there are still some browsers in use that don't support the extensions at all. Basically, a browser accesses an HTML document and does the best it can with it. If there is a tag that the browser is not programmed to support, it will ignore it and move on. As a result, Web pages that are heavily dependent on Netscape tags can look completely different at best, or completely unusable at worst, when viewed on a HTML 2.0–only browser. So you do risk the chance of alienating some users. It's just something to keep in mind.

In addition, since these extensions are not a standard, not many Web page creation tools and HTML editors currently support them, as of this writing at least.

■ WHAT DOES THIS MEAN FOR DESIGNERS?

Depending on a variety of browsers to render your design is one of the things that make the Web such a unique design environment. For this reason, designers need to keep an ear to the ground and follow trends and developments in browser software. Pay attention to new features offered by the more advanced browsers such as Netscape Navigator and Internet Explorer. Watch as the competing browsers choose to adopt them, not to adopt them, or to create their own. Make your own decision whether to use extensions and to what degree.

It also calls for the need to just *let go* of some of the control you're probably accustomed to when you design for a more fixed medium. The Web is more fluid and shifting. For me, it was one of the hardest things to get used to when starting out in this new medium.

In the beginning, I recommend viewing Web pages on as many browsers running on as many platforms as you can. You can download a fair number of them right off the Web to try out on your own machine. I used to carry around a list of some of my favorite sites that represented varying levels of complexity in their designs. Then if I happened to be visiting a friend who was running a different system than I was, I'd check out my familiar pages and see how they look. Although you can't know for sure how your page will look, you can certainly get a feel for the variations, bearing in mind that there will always be surprises and that sometimes it is impossible to make everybody happy.

Of course, there's always that user with the lime green type on a purple background.

You just have to let go.

three   assembling a web page

ELL, I THINK I'VE DONE ENOUGH explaining and describing—it's time to get down to business and actually put a Web page together, step by step. It will be a simple page, but even the most complicated pages are based on the principles described here. The point of this chapter is to demonstrate the typical Web page building process and to introduce some very basic information about HTML and graphics files. At this point, I'd like you to get a feel for the big picture; I'll be tackling the really meaty details in later chapters.

We've learned that the text portion and the graphics portion of a Web page exist separately and are brought together by a browser when a user requests the document. The design process reflects this structure and goes something like this:

- Create your HTML text document in a text editor.

- Create your graphics in a graphics program.

- Bring them together in a browser to check your work.

These steps don't need to take place in any particular order. In fact, I usually find that the order varies from project to project. Sometimes it makes sense to create my main graphics first, and then build the Web document around them. Often I'll start with a bare-bones text file and gradually embellish it with HTML tags, graphics, and features. Either way, I find I'll open my file in a browser many times throughout the process to see the effects of my additions and changes.

In the example that follows, I'll take the second approach: start with a simple text document and gradually add features such as text formatting tags and graphic files. We'll also be adding hypertext links to this document. Because they are so important, I've given the topic of creating links its very own chapter (Chapter 4, *Creating hypertext links*).

■ TOOLS, TOOLS, TOOLS

When I tell someone that I'm a Web-page designer, the first thing I'm asked is what software I use. My short answer is generally, "nothing fancy" (unless you consider Photoshop to be "fancy"; most designers consider it to be standard equipment).

Since the end result for a Web page is just a text document and some low-resolution graphics files, you don't need to go out and buy any specialized applications, the way you might if you wanted to make the leap into multimedia presentations. Needless to say, specialized applications exist, but I'll get to that later.

For my demo in this chapter, I've stuck to SimpleText to create my HTML file (although any text editor that can save plain ASCII text would do), Adobe Photoshop 3.0 to create the graphics, and Netscape as the browser for checking my work. These tools are very similar to what I actually use to create Web pages on the job. I find that it helps to have enough RAM available on your computer to be able to run all of these applications (plus a few extra utilities) at the same time.

Note that although I use a Macintosh in the following demonstration, text editors, Web browsers, and Adobe Photoshop are available for the Windows platform as well. The steps to constructing a Web page are the same regardless of the computer or specific tools you use.

Mac users should note the Internet doesn't know what a "folder" is. I've used the Macintosh terminology in this demo for consistency's sake, but on the Net, which is largely based on the UNIX operating system, the correct term is "directory." You should get used to thinking in terms of directories and subdirectories right away.

I must mention that there are new Web design tools available with drag-n-drop, WYSIWYG interfaces. These new tools enable you to design Web pages without ever seeing the HTML code that drives it (just like today you have desktop publishing tools that prevent you from having to write PostScript code). They also function like browsers, so you can see the results of your work as you go along.

These applications enable you to create your HTML file, do some limited graphics tweaking, and check your work all in one place. This capability means no bouncing between lots of applications as I do now, and that could save you a lot of time. But the end result is still the same: an HTML text file and a collection of separate graphics that rely on a browser to be seen rendered together on a page.

As of this writing, I find that the all-in-one tools lack the sophistication I need to build serious Web sites. I prefer the control I get by creating each element in a tool dedicated to doing a particular task. For now, commercial Web design tools are like asking a racecar driver to drive a car with automatic transmission. I'm sure this will change as tools are constantly updated to match designers' needs. Despite the availability of tools like these, it doesn't hurt to know all the steps of putting a Web page together "the hard way," even if it's just to gain appreciation for what Web page design software will spare you.

■ HTML AUTHORING TOOLS

There are HTML editing tools out there that will make your life a little easier. The following lists are intended only as examples of the types of tools that are available, but since the market and individual products change so rapidly, a printed book is not the appropriate medium for detailed product reviews. By no means should the list below be considered as an endorsement of any of the products listed, nor should any omissions be considered a warning. For more up-to-date information on available tools, check out the listing in Yahoo (*http://www.yahoo.com*).

HTML Editors

There is a quite a bit of HTML authoring software out there, both commercial versions and shareware programs. Generally, an HTML editor is a word processor with special tools and shortcuts for adding tags to a text file. Just highlight the text and select an item from a menu or tap on a couple of keys and presto, all the tags are inserted just right.

There are many HTML editors that can be downloaded right from the Internet for free or for some nominal fee. Some of the most popular are HTML-Editor, HTMLEdit, and BBEdit Lite with HTML extensions. Try out a few of them to see which one you like the best.

If you are interested in spending some money for a higher-powered product (and a manual), there's SoftQuad's HoTMetaL Pro, now available for the Mac.

HTML Exporters

Another class of HTML tools takes desktop publishing files and turns them into HTML files by running the elements through HTML tagging filters. These tools are convenient if you develop a magazine or newsletter for print that you'd like to also publish regularly online.

There is an HTML filter built into Adobe Pagemaker 6; Quark users can purchase an Xtension called BeyondPress; and for those setting books in FrameMaker, there's WebMaker 2.0.

These tools can be real time-savers for translating pre-formatted materials, but they don't exactly make Quark or PageMaker a viable option for Web page creation. You need to jump through so many hoops to get to the final HTML product, that it's better just to start from scratch in a non-print-biased environment.

WYSIWYG Page and Site Builders

A smattering of tools are appearing that promise to be the face of Web authoring in the future. With these tools, you won't need to fuss with HTML tags at all. Highlight a phrase and make it a heading. Want a graphic? Drag one from the desktop into place. If the graphic is too big and not properly formatted, the program will resize and convert it for you.

Adobe's PageMill has been getting large amounts of attention for making strides toward this kind of usability. Its drawbacks are that it doesn't support Netscape extensions and doesn't provide a way to directly manipulate HTML even if you want to. NaviSoft's NaviPress is another all-in-one Web page creation tool.

At the next level are tools for creating and managing entire sites. They automate the process of keeping all links between changing documents up-to-date.

Creating the HTML file

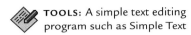

TOOLS: A simple text editing program such as Simple Text

As I discussed earlier, Web pages are just basic text files marked up with HTML tags that give the browser instructions on how to display the information and where to place elements on the page. We'll begin here by creating such a text file. In real life, it's likely that you'll begin with a pre-existing text file and won't need to start one from scratch as I am here.

Don't worry too much in this section about learning what every tag does; I'll cover tags more thoroughly in Chapter 10. For now, pay more attention to how they are used.

▪ A. CREATE A NEW TEXT DOCUMENT.

When you save the file, be sure to give it a name that ends in the suffix ".html" (or ".htm" if you're certain that your Web page will end up being served from a PC computer).

▪ B. TYPE IN THE TEXT FOR YOUR WEB PAGE.

For this demo, I'll type in a bit of non-sense and tag it up later. (Once you are comfortable with HTML, you could just type in the tags as you go along.) Or as I noted above, you may be starting with a text file and will skip this step.

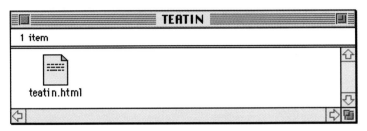

To keep this demo simple, we'll create one folder (a directory, if you're using a PC) in which we'll keep all of our files.

The Tea Tin

Welcome Tea Lovers!

For twenty years, The Tea Tin has specialized in bringing the finest teas from around the world right to your doorstep.

Now, with the power of the Internet, a satisfying cup of tea is only a few clicks away.

Choose from the following:

    Earl Gray
    Darjeeling
    Raspberry Decaffeinated

C. ADD SOME BASIC STRUCTURAL HTML TAGS.

1. First, tell the browser that the text is in HTML format by labeling the whole document as HTML. Place the "start HTML" tag **<HTML>** at the beginning of the text and the "end HTML" tag **</HTML>** at the end.

2. Create a header section by inserting start and end **<HEAD>** tags to contain information that you don't want to display in the main browser window. In this example, we're using the header space to contain our document's title (the text that appears in the top bar of most browsers). To indicate the title, use the start **<TITLE>** and end **</TITLE>** tags around the text as shown.

3. The body of your document is the material that displays in the browser's main window. To indicate the body copy, insert the start **<BODY>** and end **</BODY>** tags before and after the text as shown. (Note: be sure to keep them within the **<HTML>** tags.)

Some tags are used to ready our text for display in a browser. They define the "what goes where" part of the text display rather than "how it looks." I think of these as structural tags.

Note here that many HTML tags come in start/end pairs. The "end" tag has the same characters as the "start" tag, only it begins with a slash (/). Note also that certain tagged information can be nested within another set of tags, such as the <TITLE> tags within the pair of <HEAD> tags in the example below.

```
1 —  <HTML>
2 —  <HEAD>
     <TITLE>The Tea Tin</TITLE>
     </HEAD>
3 —  <BODY>

     Welcome Tea Lovers!

     For twenty years, The Tea Tin has specialized in bringing the finest
     teas from around the world right to your doorstep.

     Now, with the power of the Internet, a satisfying cup of tea is only
     a few clicks away.

     Choose from the following:

             Earl Gray
             Darjeeling
             Raspberry Decaffeinated

     </BODY>
     </HTML>
```

Just for kicks, I'll give you a peek at how that document would look in a browser tagged as we've left it on the previous page. If you save the file and open it in a browser, you should see something like this:

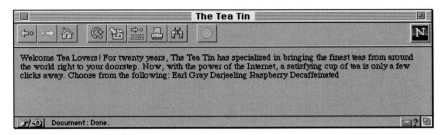

Holy smokes! What happened to my tabs and returns? One of the first things you need to know about writing HTML documents is that the only way to get a line break is to enter a tag that tells the browser to do so. Otherwise, it will just ignore returns, tabs, and consecutive spaces. That feature comes in handy, in a way, since you can enter as many returns in your HTML document as you like to make it more readable while it's in the text editor and know that it isn't affecting your final product.

Now, let's get that text into shape by adding a few tags that give text formatting instructions. Remember, you can specify that you'd like a line to be a first-level head, but you can't specify the exact font, size, etc. And again, this is not intended to be a demonstration of everything you can do with HTML text (see Chapter 10 for a more in-depth demonstration of tags), but merely an example of some of the steps in building a Web page from the ground up.

■ D. ADD TAGS TO FORMAT THE TEXT.

In the example on the right, I've made certain design decisions regarding how the text should be organized, and I've used the following tags to implement those decisions.

1. I placed start and end first-level heading tags around the text I'd like to be set as a large bold headline (**<H1>** and **</H1>**).

2. To break the paragraphs and add a little space between them, I added paragraph break tags (**<P>**).

3. To create a heading a little smaller than the first (sorry, that's as specific as you can get in HTML), I added second-level heading tags around the text (**<H2>** and **</H2>**).

4. To make the tea selections a bulleted list, I've used the unnumbered list tags to turn on (**<UL>**) and turn off (**</UL>**) the list formatting. Within those tags, I also needed to make each line a list item (**<LI>**).

■ E. SAVE YOUR DOCUMENT.

Be sure your document is named with the ".html" or ".htm" suffix. Also, make sure that the file is text-only (ASCII) with no styles applied to the text.

```
<HTML>
<HEAD>
<TITLE>The Tea Tin</TITLE>
</HEAD>
<BODY>

<H1>Welcome Tea Lovers!</H1>
<P>
For twenty years, The Tea Tin has specialized in bringing the finest
teas from around the world right to your doorstep.
<P>
Now, with the power of the Internet, a satisfying cup of tea is only
a few clicks away.
<P>
<H2>Choose from the following:</H2>

<UL>
<LI>Earl Gray
<LI>Darjeeling
<LI>Raspberry Decaffeinated
</UL>

</BODY>
</HTML>
```

1 — (points to `<H1>Welcome Tea Lovers!</H1>`)
2 — (points to `<P>`)
3 — (points to `<H2>Choose from the following:</H2>`)
4 — (points to `<UL>`)

That'll do it. Since this is our first Web page, let's take a break now to see how our page is shaping up so far. You need to save your document before opening it in a browser. You do not need to close the document window or quit your text editing application, however.

Checking your work

TOOLS: A Web browser
(Netscape is used in this example)

■ A. OPEN YOUR HTML DOCUMENT IN A BROWSER.

Launch your browser application. Choose "Open Local" (or similar wording) from the File menu and locate your file in the dialog boxes. You don't need an Internet connection to check your work on a browser. "Open Local" means that the browser is opening a file right from within your hard drive.

■ B. TAKE A LOOK!

Well, that's not a bad start. As simple as it is, this is still a true Web page, but let's make it a little more lively by adding some graphics.

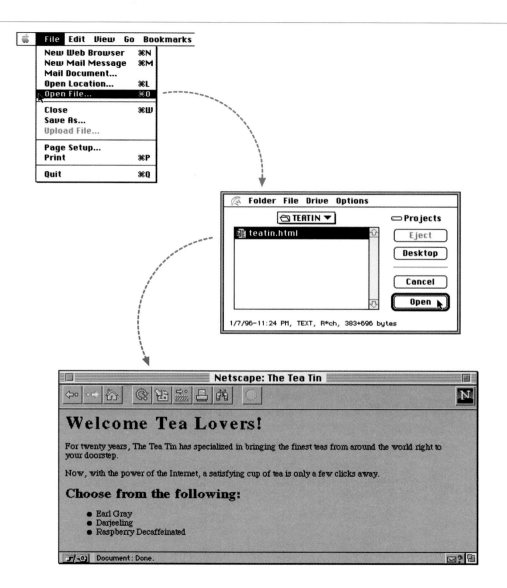

Creating graphics

TOOLS: Pixel-based graphics program (Photoshop 3.0 is used in this example)

■ A. CREATE A BANNER GRAPHIC.

First, create a new graphic file. It is important to note that the resolution is set to 72 dpi. This has become the *de facto* standard for Web graphics, although there isn't any technical reason inherent to the Internet for using 72. What's important is that the graphic be low-resolution. (See Chapter 8, *Creating better graphics,* for more on resolution issues.)

I've chosen a width of 500 pixels so it will approximately fill the top of the browser window. Since every browser on each platform has a different default width, and since users can resize a window anyway, there's no way of knowing *exactly* how wide to make a graphic to fit. It seems that most designers are creating full-width graphics somewhere in the 475-525 pixel range. There are lots of exceptions, of course.

Since this is just a quick tutorial on Web page construction, I'll save the more in-depth discussion of graphics creation for the graphics chapters (Chapters 6, 7, and 8), but for now, there are two essential little bits of information you need to know to get started.

1. The graphics must be low-resolution (i.e., 72 dpi).

2. The graphics must be in GIF format.*

That said, I'll use Photoshop** (the preference of every Web designer I've met) to create some super-simple graphics to dress up my Web page.

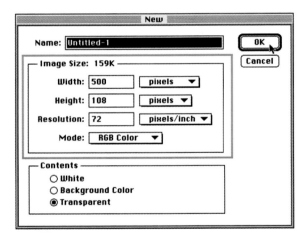

* Ah, it used to be so simple, but now we are seeing a number of browsers, following Netscape's lead, supporting other graphic file formats—JPEG being the most common to find its way onto the page layout. For this demonstration, I'll stick to GIF since it is supported by all browsers. It's just one more thing for designers to keep track of in this medium. (For more on graphic formats, see Chapter 6, *What you need to know about Web graphics.*)

**Teaching you how to use Photoshop is beyond the scope of this book, but for some useful pointers on using its functions to create Web graphics, see Chapter 7, *Creating graphics.*

B. SAVE YOUR DOCUMENT IN GIF FORMAT.

I've used the tools in Photoshop to create this simple banner for my page. It's currently a layered Photoshop 3.0 file. In order to use it on my Web page, it needs to be saved in GIF format.

1. Change the format to Indexed Color from RGB by selecting "Mode," then "Index Color" from the menu bar.

2. It will ask you whether you'd like to flatten layers. Tell it OK. (Note, I usually save a copy of my layered file before saving it as a GIF so I can go back and make those inevitable changes easily.)

3. In the Indexed Color dialog box, choose 8-bit color, which will give you 256 pixel colors. You can choose a lower bit setting to make the file size smaller. I generally choose "Adaptive" under the Palette list and "Diffusion" as the Dithering scheme (for more information on the Indexed Color dialog box, see Chapter 7).

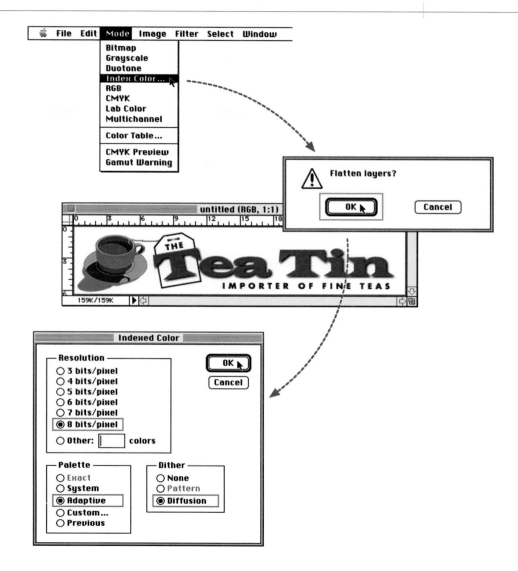

4. Choose "Save as" from the "File" menu. Locate the folder in which you'd like to save your file. In order to keep it simple for the browser to find the graphic from this HTML file, for this example, we'll save the graphic in the same folder as the HTML document.

   Be sure to name the graphic with the suffix ".gif."

   In the pull-down window next to "Format:," choose "CompuServe GIF"* from the list of file format choices. Hit OK, and your GIF is now saved and ready for your Web page.

5. I've repeated the steps above to create another simple graphic, link.gif, that will appear on my page. All the files are saved together in the TEATIN folder.

   Now that my graphics files are ready, let's plug them into my HTML file.

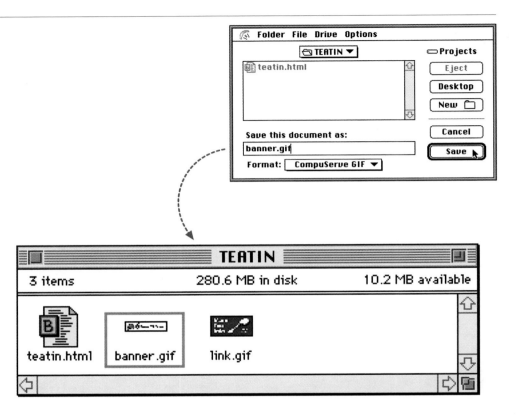

*Photoshop uses the name "CompuServe GIF" because CompuServe first developed the format, but it is just plain GIF format.

Adding graphical elements to a Web page

 TOOLS: A text editing program such as Simple Text

▨ A. ADDING THE BANNER GRAPHIC

I'd like my page to have a banner centered at the top.

Use image tags to plug graphics into the HTML document. For example, to place my banner graphic at the top of my page, I entered the following tag:

```
<IMG SRC="banner.gif">
```

When a browser encounters an <IMG...> tag, it interprets it as "place graphic here." It then looks within the tag for more information such as the name of the graphic. The portion of the tag

```
...SRC="banner.gif"
```

tells the browser that the source is a graphic called *banner.gif.* Because the graphic is located in the same directory as our HTML file, there is no need to print the entire directory path name to get to it. We are describing where to find the graphic *relative* to the HTML file. (For more about relative pathnames and URLs, see Chapter 4.)

By default, all the elements on Web pages are aligned flush left, ragged right, but I can center a graphic by placing the start centering, <CENTER>, tag before the graphic tag, and the end centering, </CENTER>, tag right after it. (The centering tag can be used around text as well.)

```
<HTML>

<HEAD>
<TITLE>The Tea Tin
</TITLE>
</HEAD>

<BODY>
<CENTER><IMG SRC="banner.gif"></CENTER>
<P>
<H1>Welcome Tea Lovers</H1>
<P>
<IMG SRC="link.gif" ALT="For more tea information" ALIGN=left
HSPACE=6 VSPACE=3 BORDER=0 > For twenty years, The Tea Tin has
specialized in bringing the finest teas from around the world right to
your doorstep.
<P>
Now, with the power of the Internet, a satisfying cup of tea is only a few
clicks away.
<P>
<HR>
<P>
<H2>Choose from the following:</H2>

<UL>
<LI>Earl Gray
<LI>Darjeeling
<LI>Raspberry Decaffeinated
</UL>

</BODY>
</HTML>
```

B. ADD A SECOND GRAPHIC.

In the first example, we added the source information for which graphic to use right within the <IMG> tag itself. You can also put other display instructions within an image tag.

I'd like my second graphic to be displayed on the left edge of the screen with text wrapping around it. By default (and as far as you can go with HTML 2.0), graphics are set flush left with only one line of text next to them, usually base-aligned with the graphic image. The rest of the area next to the graphic is left blank. I've added some display information to the <IMG> tag to override that default. Note that the tags for these attributes are added right within the <IMG> tag itself, separated only by spaces.

Let's take a look at the parts of the image tag.

<IMG...>
> says "place graphic file here."

...SRC="utensils.gif"
> tells the browser to use the graphic called utensils.gif which is in the same directory as the HTML file.

ALT="(text)"
> the text within this portion of the image tag will display in the browser window if the graphic itself cannot be displayed.

ALIGN=left*
> aligns the graphic on the left edge of the browser and allows multiple lines of text to wrap around it.

HSPACE=6*
> creates a gutter of some number of blank pixels (6 in our example) to the left and right of the graphic so the text doesn't butt right up against it.

VSPACE=3*
> creates a gutter of some number of blank pixels (3 in our example) above and below the graphic so the graphic doesn't crash into the lines of text above and below.

BORDER=0*
> when graphics are used as links to other documents, browsers put a distinctive blue line around them. This tag tells the browsers that understand it to turn that border off.

*These tags are not part of the HTML 2.0 standard; therefore, this tag may not be supported by all browsers.

C. ADD A HORIZONTAL RULE.

I've also decided that it might be nice to have a line separating my list of recipes from the introductory text.

The <HR> tag tells the browser to "draw a horizontal rule here." Since the browser is generating this rule according to its defaults, the way it will look to the user is dependent on the browser he or she is using. You can be sure only that there will be a horizontal divider there of some sort.

Note that I've added paragraph tags, <P>, above and below the rule to add a little extra space around it, but this is optional.

D. SAVE!

I'd like to see the results of my efforts, so I'll save this HTML file and open it in the browser to see how it looks.

Checking your work

TOOLS: A Web browser (Netscape Navigator is used in this example)

A. OPEN OR RELOAD YOUR HTML DOCUMENT IN A BROWSER.

Follow the steps on page 31 in this chapter to open the improved HTML file in a browser, or reload the document if your browser is already open and displaying the older version of the document. To reload, choose Reload from the File menu of your browser. *Command-R* is a typical keystroke shortcut to do the same thing, or you can use the reload button on the browser toolbar.

Be sure that you've saved your HTML document and all your graphics files before you try to view them.

B. TAKE A LOOK!

The Tea Tin may not be the fanciest home page on the Web, but the essentials are all there.

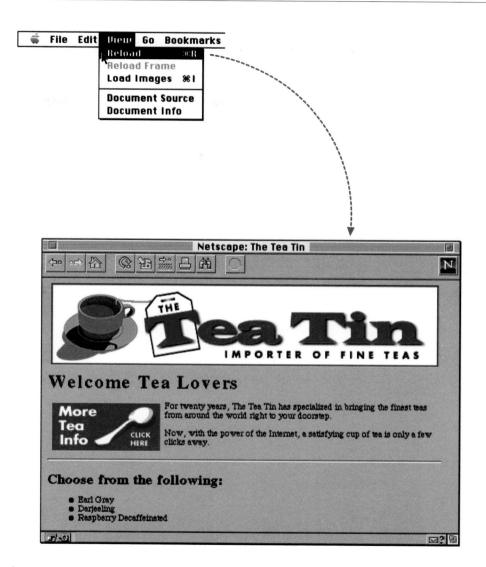

CACHING

When browsing the Web, it's typical to move back and forth between documents, often returning to the same document repeatedly. It doesn't make sense for the browser to ask a server for the same document over and over again, so instead browsers retain a copy of the most recently accessed documents and images so they have it handy in case you want to return to it. This is called *caching*, and the place these files are temporarily stored is called the *cache*.

The benefit to you is that you don't have to wait for the document to download each time, just for the browser to reformat the file from the cache. The only disadvantage is that if the original document on the server has changed, the browser doesn't always know, so you have to explicitly tell the browser to reload the document (i.e., ask the server for the Web page all over again).

You can take advantage of the browser's caching capability by reusing the same graphic whenever possible on the pages of your site. It will only need to be downloaded once and will speed up the display of subsequent pages.

A FEW COMMON PROBLEMS

When I teach classes on Web page design, the same simple problems seem to occur for people during their first time through the process of putting together a Web page. I thought I'd answer the most common questions here in case you encounter similar difficulties.

1. I changed my Web page document, but I don't see my changes in the browser.

   You need to reload the document in the browser, or it will continue to display the last version. For more information, see the sidebar on caching on this page.

2. I've made some changes to my Web page, but when I reload it in the browser, it looks exactly the same.

   One reason could be that you didn't save your HTML document before reloading. It's an important step.

3. My graphics are showing up as little generic icons on the page.

   This means that the browser sees an image tag, but is unable to load in the graphic file. This can happen for a number of reasons.

   ■ *Your graphic was not saved in Compuserve GIF format. Open it in the graphics program and be sure to save it in the correct format.*

   ■ *The name of your graphic is not* exactly *the same as the name you specified in the image tag in your HTML file. Double check the text after* "SRC=".

   ■ *Your graphic is not in the right place. Be sure that if the graphic is in a sub-folder (or subdirectory), the complete and correct pathname is listed after* "SRC=" *in the image tag. For more on subdirectories, see Chapter 4.*

   ■ *Graphics may be turned off in your browser. For example, in Netscape you may have "auto-download images" turned off. Make sure this option is selected.*

4. The text in my entire document is really huge and black.

   Make sure that all your headings tag contain the end tag (for example, </H1>), or the browser will continue to display your file in large, bold text. It's easy to miss closing tags, even for experienced taggers.

5. My graphic is *huge* and runs way off the page.

   Your graphic is probably in a resolution that is too high. In the print world, it is typical to have resolutions as high as 300 or 600 dots per inch. For the Web, I recommend creating graphics at (or converting them to) a resolution of 72 dpi. For more information on resolution issues, see Chapter 6.

four creating hypertext links

F YOU'RE CREATING A PAGE FOR THE WEB, chances are you don't intend it to exist in isolation. But you'll want it to point to other Web pages, whether to another section of your own site or to someone else's. Linking, after all, is what the Web is all about.

If you've used the Web at all, you should be familiar with the highlighted text and graphics that beg, "click me!" There is one tag that makes this linking possible, the *anchor* tag, which is used like this:

<A HREF=" *(URL)* " > *text or graphic to be linked* </A>

Let's look at the parts of this tag:

<A ...> and **</A>**
The anchor tag is one of those on/off paired tags that we've seen in previous examples, so you are telling the browser to "start hypertext link" and "end hypertext link." You can turn any graphic or any string of text on your page into a link. Be sure to include all the tags—and all the parts of those tags—associated with the selected text or graphic within the anchor tags.

... HREF=" *(URL)* **"**
In addition, you need to say what document you wish to link to by specifying its URL (its address on the Web). This information is specified within the "start" portion of the tag. It is similar to the "**SRC=**" part of the <IMG> tag that tells the browser what graphic to use and where to get it.

Let's add some links to our ever-improving (and growing!) HTML file for the Tea Tin site.

Linking to a document out on the Web

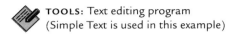 **TOOLS:** Text editing program
(Simple Text is used in this example)

```
<HTML>
<HEAD>
<TITLE>The Tea Tin</TITLE>
</HEAD>
<BODY>

<CENTER><IMG SRC="banner.gif"></CENTER>
<P>
<H1>Welcome Tea Lovers</H1>
<P>
<A HREF="http://vtek.chalmers.se/~v92tilma/tea/teapage.html"><IMG
SRC="link.gif" ALIGN=left HSPACE=6 VSPACE=3 BORDER=0></A> For
twenty years, The Tea Tin has specialized in bringing the finest teas
from around the world right to your doorstep.
...
</BODY>
</HTML>
```

■ ABSOLUTE URLS

In my example, I'd like to make the small graphic a link to a popular list of other cooking resources on the Web. To do this, I've started by adding the anchor tag around the <IMG> tag.

Notice that I've told the browser exactly where to link to by typing in the complete (or absolute) URL for that page. The absolute URL contains the following elements:

1. protocol

2. host name

3. path

4. file name

With the long URL pathname and the long <IMG> tag, the string of code can look pretty confusing, but structurally it's as simple as the example in the introduction to this section.

Linking to a document on your own site

▪ RELATIVE URLS

To make each title a link, I've added the start and end anchor tags before and after the name of the tea. But look at the URL I've specified this time:

```
HREF="earlgray.html"
```

It looks incomplete compared to our last example, but it will work, because what we're doing here is pointing the browser to a filename *relative* to the position of the HTML file it's currently displaying. In other words, we don't need to use all the parts of an absolute link (parts 1, 2, and 3 shown on the previous page) since we're not asking the browser to go into another directory.

Without the rest of the URL specified, the browser will assume the same HTTP protocol, host name, and directory path. It will simply look in the same directory as the current HTML file for the file it's supposed to link to.

*Technically, the HTML specifications don't allow links to be embedded within lists. This fact doesn't prevent people from doing it anyway since browsers generally handle the information just fine.

o keep the tea page clean and simple, I decided to list only the names of the types of teas and to make them links to complete information on separate pages.* But before we start tagging, let's take a look at the files that make up the Tea Tin Web site.

While you weren't looking, I followed the steps on pages 27–30 in Chapter 3 to tag up a page for each tea on my list and then saved them in the same directory as my other files for this site.

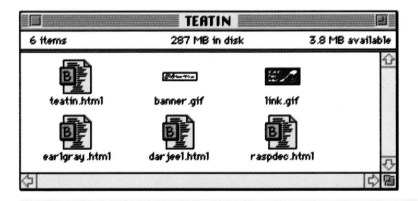

```
...
<H2>Choose from the following:</H2>

<UL>
<LI><A HREF="earlgray.html">Earl Gray</A>
<LI><A HREF="darjeel.html">Darjeeling</A>
<LI><A HREF="raspdec.html">Raspberry Decaffeinated</A>
</UL>

</BODY>
</HTML>
```

If the file is on the same server but in a different directory, you may need to include some path information in the relative URL. Let's reorganize our files a bit to see how this works.

Say this grew to be a *huge* catalog with hundreds of types of tea for sale. At a certain point, it gets confusing to keep all the files for a complex site in a single directory, so it's a good idea to create subdirectories.

In this example, I've created a new directory within TEATIN, called TEAS, to store all of my tea HTML files. Now let's take a look at the anchor tag that links the titles to their respective recipes:

HREF="TEAS/earlgray.html"

The new tag tells the browser to look in the current directory for a subdirectory called TEAS and in that directory for a file called *earlgray.html*.

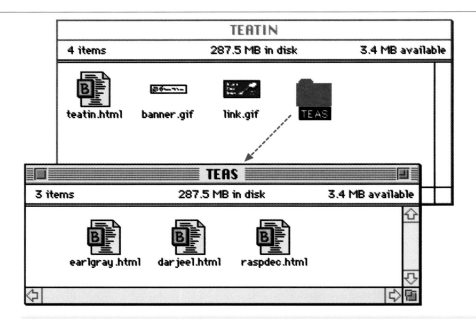

```
...
<H2>Choose from the following:</H2>

<UL>
<LI><A HREF="TEAS/earlgray.html">Earl Gray</A>
<LI><A HREF="TEAS/darjeel.html">Darjeeling</A>
<LI><A HREF="TEAS/raspdec.html">Raspberry Decaffeinated</A>
</UL>

</BODY>
</HTML>
```

Relative URLs are also commonly used in image (<IMG>) tags.

Remember in our sample <IMG> tag, we specified SRC="banner.gif"... that was actually a *relative* URL that told the browser to look in the current directory and place the graphic called *banner.gif* on the page.

I find it quite useful to keep all my graphics in a subdirectory called "graphics" then use a relative URL in the image tag to point to it:

```
<IMG SRC="graphics/banner.gif " >.
```

Using relative URLs to point to your own files is just an option, not a necessity. Using the absolute URL would have worked just as well, but relative URLs give you a couple of advantages. One is that if you want to make changes to your site, you are able to move a whole directory to a new location without having to change the path-name in every single link and image tag. The other is that they are much simpler to use and quicker to type.

Being able to use relative pathnames correctly and confidently means gaining a familiarity with UNIX syntax for movement through directory trees. If you will be responsible for creating the HTML files for complex Web sites, you might want to take the time to read more about it in an introductory UNIX book, such as *Learning the UNIX Operating System,* published by O'Reilly & Associates, Inc.

On the following page let's take one last look at the Tea Tin home page in its final incarnation.

Checking your work

TOOLS: A Web browser (Netscape Navigator is used in this example)

A. OPEN OR RELOAD YOUR HTML DOCUMENT IN A BROWSER OR RELOAD THE DOCUMENT.

B. TAKE A LOOK!

My text links now have their tell-tale blue coloring and in this case, underlining. Not all browsers will display links the same way. Some will use underlines, some won't. With extensions, you can specify the color in which you'd like the links to appear for those folks using the Netscape browser or Internet Explorer.

C. CLICK AWAY!

Test your links by clicking on them. If you did it correctly, the browser should retrieve the linked file.

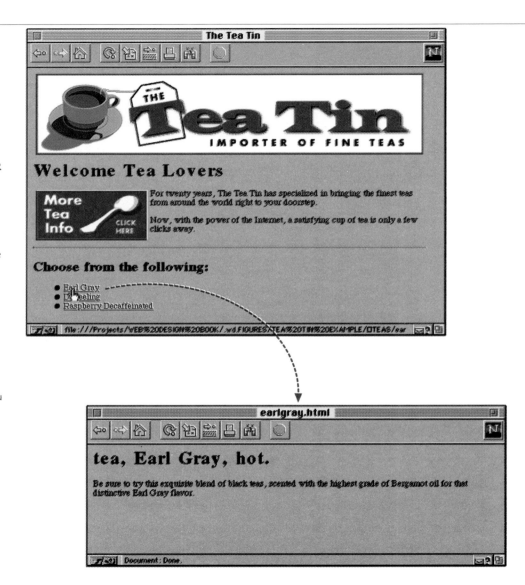

five   new considerations for a new medium

OW THAT YOU MADE IT THROUGH the last four chapters, you should have a basic understanding of how the Web works and how a Web page is put together. Throughout, I have tried to point out some of the peculiarities of the medium, but I'd like to sum it up one last time. It's important to have a feel for the landscape before you set out.

■ 1. KEEP DOWNLOAD TIMES IN MIND.

Remember that a Web page is published over a network, and it will need to go zipping through the lines as little bundles of data in order to reach the end user. It should be fairly intuitive, then, that larger amounts of data will require a longer time to get there. And guess which part of a Web page is the greatest hog of bandwidth—that's right, the graphics. Simply put, large graphics mean long download times.

Thus is born the love/hate relationship with graphics on the Web. On the one hand, it has been the ability to display pictures along with text that has made the Web the first portion of the Internet to explode into mass popularity. But on the other hand, they can also try the patience of the eager surfer, waiting, waiting, waiting for the pictures to download and display on the screen.

The user has three choices: hang in there and wait for everything to appear as it was intended to be viewed, turn the graphics-downloading function of the browser off and just read the HTML text, or stop downloading altogether and move on to another Web page.

■ HOW LONG WILL IT TAKE?

It's impossible to say just how long a graphic will take to download over the Web since it's dependent on so many factors. These factors include the speed of the user's connection to the Net, the browser making the request, the amount of activity on the server, and the general amount of traffic on the Internet itself.

Because the graphics on the Web are very low resolution, their file sizes aren't that big to begin with compared to graphics in the print world; they tend to range between one and 100K (I try to keep mine under 30K).

I've seen a 30K graphic load virtually instantly over a good Internet connection such as a 56K or T1 line. I've seen that same graphic take 2 minutes or even longer over a 14.4 kbps modem (and that's a long time to stare at an empty screen).

Many people use the formula of two seconds per graphic plus one second per "K" just to get a ballpark estimate for how long the graphic will take to load (that would be thirty seconds for a 28K graphic). Under the best of conditions, it could be an instant. Under the worst, it could take many times longer.

Does that help?

Many users are additionally handicapped by accessing Web pages over slow modem connections. You are especially at risk of losing this portion of the Internet audience— and it's a large portion— if you do not take measures to keep your file sizes as small as possible.

The very nature of publishing over a network creates a new responsibility for designers to be sensitive to the issue of download times. When I design for print, a really enormous graphic file means only a possible inconvenience for me and the folks outputting my files to film. On the Web, large graphics could mean the difference between a reader spending time at my site or bailing out before the first screen even appears.

Deciding how graphically-rich to make your page

In Chapter 8, *Creating better graphics*, I will discuss some methods for keeping the file size of your graphics in check. For now, note that there is a trade-off here that requires a new type of design decision. You must decide where your Web page falls on the spectrum between plain text-only Web pages, which download in a flash, and very elaborate Web pages with full-screen, full-color graphics that could take several minutes to display.

Largely, the decision will depend on what type of site you're designing. You wouldn't design a 4-color, die-cut, and embossed "WET PAINT" sign, because the point of that document is to get information out fast; it doesn't need to be fancy. Similarly, Web sites whose purpose is to distribute basic information quickly can be a lot more simple than sites that are aiming to create a rich online experience.

Think about how your site is going to be used, who is likely to be using it, and over what kind of Net connection. Then tailor the abundance of graphics to what you feel that audience is willing to wait for.

Providing a text-only version

A common response to this dilemma has been for publishers on the Web to provide two versions of their site, one fully-designed as they intend it to be seen, the other text-only or with very light graphical treatment for those people who have slower connections or who just want to get to the content.

Maintaining two parallel Web sites can require extra work, but it seems to be a fair response to the download time issue. The full-graphical version is available for those who have the means or patience to use it. The publisher doesn't need to make apologies for the size of the graphics because it has considered the needs of its entire audience. Most importantly, the user is given a choice of how to spend his or her time without being forced to wait.

Creating two parallel Web sites is a good way to be sympathetic to your audience, but it is by no means a solution to the bandwidth problem. For that reason, it's always desirable to take measures to keep your file sizes as small as possible without sacrificing quality. Faster downloading graphics make for a more enjoyable experience online.

Since you know a Web page is designed to travel, do your best to see that it travels light.

■ 2. KEEP THE LOWEST COMMON DENOMINATOR IN MIND.

When you design for the Web, bear in mind that not everyone out there is equipped with the best browsers running on a souped-up computer system over a lightning-fast Internet connection. Although it's good to take advantage of the latest features in Web publishing, you also have to design with a mind towards those who are viewing the Web under less than optimal conditions.

As I pointed out in Chapter 2, not everyone will see your graphics. Many people, because of the type of Internet connection they have, are stuck with a text-only browser such as Lynx. Others, because they are accessing the Web via a slow modem connection, will turn the graphics downloading off so they can at least get to the information.

Granted, these folks are not getting the whole Web experience, but for them I do my best to ensure that my Web pages are at least *functional*. By functional, I mean that the page is still able to communicate its primary message and that it provides the same, or similar, navigational choices that you'd find on the graphical page. No page should be a complete dead-end when the graphics aren't displayed.

Use ALT text

In my sample Web page, I'd like users with non-graphical browsers to know that the banner graphic contains the headline to my page, "The Tea Tin." HTML provides a way to substitute a bit of text in the place of a missing graphic. You do this with the ALT tag. Actually, it's not a tag on its own, but rather another attribute that you can add within an image (<IMG>) tag. So, to make sure all users can see the title of my page, graphics or not, I'd add the alternative text information to the image tag in this way:

```
<IMG SRC="banner.gif" ALT="The Tea Tin">
```

If for some reason a browser can't display the image, it will display the text it finds after the ALT portion of the image tag. Instead of the graphic, the user will see something like this in its place:

or like this on Lynx:

Not pretty, granted, but it does communicate, which is the whole point, right? You can use ALT text to repeat the words found in a graphic, or you can use it just to describe an image. For instance, a little description like "Jane President's Portrait" is a little more rewarding than just seeing that generic graphic icon or the word IMAGE alone.

There seems to be a convention on the Web to put all ALT text in brackets [ ]. I'm not sure why this is, perhaps a carryover from when the Web was generated by programmers. I've created my own convention of using brackets only when the ALT text is describing an image, but not when it is an exact replacement of the text within the graphic. I've heard some Webmasters say that you *have to* use brackets, but really, it is up to you.

In summary, considering the capabilities of different browsers is crucial, especially when deciding to take advantage of advanced functions, such as background patterns, animation, or tables, that work only on one browser or one platform. Think about what's going to show up on browsers that don't support the tags you've implemented. Does that make your page just a little less attractive, or totally unusable? Is there anything you can do to ensure that the site is still functional and still communicates its main message to these users?

■ 3. KNOW YOUR PAGE WILL LOOK DIFFERENT.

The thing about the Web that makes it different than designing for any other medium is the lack of control you have over the final product. In Chapter 2, we saw how the look of your page can vary on every browser and according to the tastes of each individual user.

Also, the very nature of the HTML tagging system prevents us from specifying all those font-related things we're accustomed to defining. You may find this extremely frustrating, or if you've always been irked by having to decide how many points of space to put above paragraphs, you may feel extremely liberated!

Test!

The best you can do under these conditions is to get a general feel for the range of variation. You do this by testing. Try viewing your HTML document and graphics in the following situations:

- with Netscape or a browser supporting similar functions

- with that same browser running on other platforms (it may have different functionality or handle the alignment of page elements differently)

- with an HTML 2.0-only browser

- with a text-only browser

- with your browser window set to different widths and lengths (be sure to check the extremes)

- on a 14-inch monitor (you may decide that it's important that all the crucial information fits into that first screenful without a lot of scrolling)

- in gray scale, in black and white (can you still read the important text in your graphics?)

You may find that after enough testing, you'll begin to develop a mental picture of how your page will look under different circumstances, and you may only need to run a couple of the tests listed above for each new design. It's that feeling that comes with experience, like knowing how a certain ink will be likely to look when printed on a particular paper stock.

Designing for the Web involves letting go of many of your past concerns (of course, there are plenty of new ones!). Consider your audience. Do your best to construct your page to cater to their needs and the abilities or limitations of the tools they may be using. At a certain point, though, you just leave it up to fate.

Total control

If you find you can't bear the uncertainty, and you insist that readers view your page *exactly* as you carefully crafted it, there is technology available just for you. Adobe has developed Acrobat, a sort of streamlined PostScript format. Acrobat saves not only the text of a file, but all of the style and layout information necessary to display it again "just so" on the users' end.

With Acrobat, you save your page as a PDF (Portable Document Format) file. That file can be accessed via a hypertext link and downloaded just like a graphic or sound file. The user needs to have a special PDF-file viewer to look at your file,* but when it does display, it looks just the way the designer designed it; you can even zoom in to look at the details or print the page. The downside is that it is proprietary technology, meaning you need Adobe's products to view PDF files and to create them, and although the viewer is free, you will need to pay for the software necessary to create PDFs.

Portable electronic files are not a substitute for HTML, and sinking all your pages into PDFs is not exactly "Web design," but it is an available alternative for heavily formatted documents that simply *must* look a certain way or are intended to be printed on the other end. It's good to know about, but since it isn't really an inherent feature of Web page construction, I won't go into much more detail in this book. For more information on Acrobat, look at *http://www.adobe.com/Acrobat/,* Adobe's Web page on the subject .

* There is now a plug-in to Netscape which enables it to display PDF files right within the browser window, without the use of an external viewer.

■ 4. FIND CREATIVE SOLUTIONS FOR MAKING THE MOST OF A LIMITED SET OF TOOLS

Remember the scene from *Apollo 13* where the engineers were given a pile of junk thrown on a table and told they had to create a contraption from it that would save the Apollo crew's lives? That's kind of what it's like designing with HTML. If you are the sort that enjoys the problem-solving nature of design, the Web is the place for you!

Despite all the added features and extensions, HTML remains a pretty limited tool to design with (actually, it was never intended to be a *design* tool to begin with). By nature of the technology, graphics can be used only in so many ways, and there aren't many options for displaying text. As I said before, there are only about a dozen or so tags that will do most of the work you need to do.

In an interesting way, this limitation serves to level the playing field. Large Fortune 500 companies with gargantuan budgets have the same short list of tags to work with as a college student throwing together a personal home page in a computer lab. As with any good design, what it comes down to is ingenuity.

In spite of the limitations, truly unique and exciting Web page designs are popping up every day. Thank goodness for the menu option "View Source" to find out "how did they *do* that?!" The trick is to turn those limitations into a challenge and see what you can build.*

■ 5. FOLLOW EMERGING TECHNOLOGIES

I suppose this isn't exactly a *new* concern. Since the birth of desktop publishing, designers have felt the pressures of keeping up with the latest tools and technologies. Nowhere is this more true than in the world of Web design, where new software for creating Web pages and viewing them appears weekly, and major advances in technology occur every few months.

The area where I feel it's most important to keep your finger on the pulse is browser technology. As I mentioned in Chapter 2, *More about browsers*, it's the browser that ultimately determines how a Web page is rendered, and designers are at the mercy of developers and their new standards. But they can also influence the outcome by casting

*The downside is that a lot of Web pages are created out of ingenious fudges and downright bogus HTML, using the tags in a way that is illegal according to the rules of HTML. I'm an advocate of clean HTML files, that use the tags as they were intended to be used. That means no sinking a list within a list within a list in order to sort of achieve the effect of centering. You can still find innovative uses for tags and the features they produce without using them incorrectly.

votes in the form of using features that are useful and make sense, or by ridiculing the obnoxious and gratuitous.

Netscape introduced an extension called <BLINK>, which causes the line of text to flash on and off. Although many people have put it to use, it was heavily criticized by most of the Web community, designers in particular. Not surprisingly, it's one of the Netscape extensions that is not finding its way into other browsers that are beginning to support some of the other Netscape tags.

If you do not have access to the Internet, you can pick up trade magazines such as *Internet World* or *WebWeek* to keep up with the latest. If you are online, you can read newsgroups such as *comp.infosystems.www.authoring.html*. Yahoo, an index of just about everything on the Web, organized by subject, is also a great source for technical Web information. Point your browser at *http://www.yahoo.com*, then look within "Computers & Internet" for "World Wide Web." From there, you are sure to find enough new information to keep you busy.

It's a good idea to regularly check the Web pages of the companies such as Netscape that are developing the new technology and standards. You'll find they're more than happy to provide the information you need right on their pages.

If you see an effect on a Web page that you like, be sure to view the source file to see how it was created. Even better, send some email to the person who designed it (there's nearly always a contact name and address listed at each site) and make friends. There are few enough designers on the Web right now that I've found it to be a fun and supportive community.

I also can't recommend highly enough that you find yourself at least one "geek" friend who lives and breathes this Web stuff, spending his or her life following the trends and digging up the hottest new shareware. Take this friend out to lunch regularly in exchange for news from the front. Be forewarned: in this business you are at serious risk of becoming a geek yourself. I have, and I'm proud of it!

all about graphics
for the web

what you need to know about web graphics

K, HERE'S WHAT YOU NEED TO KNOW:

Inline images need to be low-resolution graphics saved in the GIF format.

This tidy sentence basically says it all, but you'd probably feel a little ripped off if I just left it at that. Instead, I'd like to use the above statement as a starting point for discussing some of the nuts and bolts of Web graphics. Although simple, the statement touches on some major issues that I'll explore in this chapter: using graphics online, graphic formats, and image resolution.

■ HOW YOU CAN USE GRAPHICS

Graphics are be displayed on the Web in three basic ways. *Inline* images appear in the browser window as the HTML file is displayed. Other graphics are displayed only when a reader clicks on a link, and they may be displayed in a window separate from the Web page itself. A graphic file can also be used as a tiled background pattern by some browsers.

Inline images

What do I mean by *inline*? Inline images are the graphics that you see displayed along with the HTML-formatted text in the browser window. Every graphic that is placed in the line of HTML text using the <IMG> tag is an inline image, including every banner, button, and decorative image you see on the Web page. An inline image can be used a number of ways:

1. As a decoration

   Inline images are commonly used just to give life to an otherwise lifeless, text-filled page. You can use them to contain the title of your Web page, the company's logo, or a picture of the President's cat.

   A graphic is placed inline by adding an image tag to the HTML document as shown below. (See Chapter 3 for an introduction to image tags or Chapter 10, *Creating imagemaps*, for more complete tag information.)

   ```
   <IMG SRC="name.gif">
   ```

2. As a link to a document

   Graphics can serve as hyperlinks to other documents as an alternative to text links. Place anchor tags around the image tag, just as you would around a string of text characters you'd want to link:

   ```
   <A HREF="document.html"><IMG SRC="name.gif"></A>
   ```

   In standard HTML 2.0, when a graphic is linked, it is surrounded by a bright blue line.* (See page 36 in Chapter 3 for how to turn it off using Netscape extensions.)

3. As a link to multiple documents

   A single graphic can serve as a link to many HTML documents by creating clickable "hotspots" within the image area. Where the user links depends on what area of the image he or she clicks on. These graphics are known as *imagemaps*, *imagemapped graphic*s, or sometimes just *ismap*s. Since an imagemap is linked, it will be adorned by the tell-tale blue outline, unless you turn it off.

   Creating imagemapped graphics isn't as simple as adding a single tag to the HTML file. The complete process is outlined in detail in Chapter 10, *Creating imagemaps*.

Images accessed with links

If you don't want a graphic to appear inline on your Web page, but you still want to make it available to your audience, you can create a link to that graphic from some text or a graphic in the HTML document.

* Blue is the conventional default color for indicating a link, although it is another factor determined by the browser settings. In addition, there are extensions to HTML that allow the Web page designer to specify a different color for links.

■ HELPER APPLICATIONS

In addition to graphics files, you can build links to sound, video, Adobe Acrobat, and even multimedia files from within a Web page. Most browsers rely on external viewers or players, also known as "helper applications," to interpret and play or display the files.

The trend in browsers, led by Netscape, is to incorporate these functions right into the browser by means of specialized plug-ins. Like plug-ins to Adobe Photoshop, which you might be familiar with, browser plug-ins by third party developers expand the browser's functionality.

The tagging is the same as for any other link, except that the URL points to a graphic file instead of an HTML document:

```
<A HREF="big.jpeg">Click here for JPEG</A>
```

The graphic will only be displayed when the reader clicks on that link. Exactly how it is displayed depends on the format of the graphic and the browser trying to display it, but generally, it will appear on a separate page or window from the Web page that linked to it.

If the graphic is readable by the browser, it will load right into the current (or perhaps a new) browser window. If it is in a format that the browser can't display, JPEG format being the most common, the browser will turn to a "helper application" to do the displaying.

For instance, in the example above I've linked to a graphic that was saved in the JPEG format (you can tell by the .jpeg or .jpg suffix). If my browser doesn't support JPEGs, it launches a utility such as JPEGView, and the image appears there (Figure 6-1).

With Netscape Navigator, users can choose between having the browser either launch an external viewer for JPEGs or display the image right in the browser window.

FIGURE 6-1 ▶
*A browser using JPEGView to display
a graphic in JPEG format*

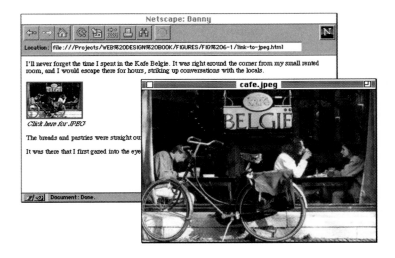

Why link to a graphic?

If you had a series of very large graphics with jumbo file sizes, whether in JPEG or GIF format, you might decide (and wisely so) to provide links to these images instead of forcing them to download as inline images on a page. One convention Web page designers use is a postage stamp size image that links to the respective full-size version. Obviously not all graphics should be hidden from view, but for certain applications—such as a catalog of travel photos, book covers, or fine art prints—this method is the way to go.

Background graphics

The third way a graphic can be used online is as a tile in a tiled background image. If you've spent any time perusing the Web using Netscape, you've most likely seen tiled backgrounds ranging from subtle and textural to obnoxious and chaotic (Figure 6-2).

FIGURE 6-2 ▶
Examples of acceptable and unacceptable tiled backgrounds

Like most effects on the Web, the secret to tiling lies in the HTML file. At the risk of getting ahead of myself, I'll share the tag with you now since I brought it up.

To use a graphic as a tile background, add the following information within the <BODY> tag at the beginning of the document:

```
<BODY BACKGROUND="tile.gif">
```

A word of warning: background tiles are difficult to use well. Remember that your HTML text needs to be read *over* the pattern, and a background pattern that is too busy or full of contrast can make the text virtually illegible.

Also, bear in mind that backgrounds that look light and subtle on your souped-up, 24-bit designer monitor (if you're so lucky) can look drastically different (read "awful") on lesser monitors and on other platforms. I created a tile based on a scan of craft paper for the cover of *Web Review*. On my monitor, it is a soft, even-toned tan color, yet I continue to receive email from users who complain that my text was completely unreadable over that "burnt orange background with red dots." It's another unknown to keep in mind when you design and one more reason to test!

■ GRAPHIC FILE FORMATS

Kiss your TIFF and EPS files goodbye! The Web has its own alphabet soup of graphics file formats. Graphics formats that make it on the Internet are those that are easily ported from platform to platform over a network. The file formats that have made the grade on the Web tend to be the most generic and compact formats available.

GIF

The GIF (Graphic Interchange Format) file is the traditional darling of the Internet. Whether you pronounce it "Gif" or "Jif" is your call (there are polls on the Net where you can cast your vote; I find I tend to switch between the two at random).

GIF files are compressed files that can contain a maximum of 8-bit color information. By compressed, I mean that in turning your graphic into a GIF file, you are running it through a process that squeezes the color information into the smallest file size that can contain it. "8-bit color" means that the graphic can contain a maximum of 256 different pixel colors. (See the sidebar on page 70 in Chapter 7 for more information on bit depth.)

Before you can save a graphic in GIF format, you need to reduce the number of colors that appear in it by changing it to what Adobe calls "Indexed Color." In Photoshop, you do this by changing the Mode to "Indexed Color" and selecting the number of colors you'd like. The default is 8-bit, but you can select fewer if you choose. If the image is not in Indexed Color mode, the "CompuServe GIF" format will not be available to you when you save the file. For a more detailed demonstration of how to save a GIF from within Photoshop, see pages 32–34 in Chapter 3; for more info on Indexed Color, see pages 69–72 in Chapter 7.

JPEG

The second most popular graphics format on the Web today is the JPEG format. The advantages to graphics saved in JPEG format are that they are in 24-bit color (that's millions of pixel colors), and the compression is much more efficient for photographic images.* Although the compression scheme is "lossy," meaning the image quality after compression is some degree worse than the original, JPEGs still offer better image quality packed into smaller files. The answer to many Web designers' prayers, right? Well, not entirely.

Unfortunately, although Netscape Navigator and some other browsers** can display JPEGs as inline images, many other browsers still do not. If you use all JPEGs for inline images, you run the risk of making your page useless to a portion of your potential audience.

So, I should clarify the statement that opened this chapter by saying that inline graphics must be in GIF format *to be universally supported by all graphical browsers.*

And there's more!

The ART compression scheme developed by Johnson-Grace for the America Online interface is on the verge of making its Internet debut. The word is that ART graphics will be supported as inline images in an upcoming release of Netscape and are already supported by the AOL and GNN browsers. Whether other browsers will follow suit remains to be seen.

And if that's not bad enough, there is yet another graphic file format optimized for the Web called the Portable Network Graphic, or PNG, format. PNG is a non-proprietary

*See pages 82–85 in Chapter 8 for file size comparisons between GIF and JPEG.

**GNN, Spyglass Mosaic, NCSA Mosaic for Windows, and Internet Explorer as of this writing, with Mosaic for Macintosh and AOL's browser not far behind.

graphic format that is struggling with the standards approval process to be adopted as *the* graphic file format for the Web. Its advantages are that it is a lossless compression scheme, can support millions of colors, compresses smaller than GIF, and is an open standard. Again, we'll have to wait to see which browsers will begin supporting PNG files.

Emerging graphic format standards (and which browsers will support them) is just another example of the type of technical information serious Web designers need to pay attention to. The long and the short of it is, for the time being, if you want to be absolutely sure your graphic is seen by everyone—stick with GIF!

■ IMAGE RESOLUTION

All graphics formats supported by the Web are pixel-based, or "rasterized," images. A GIF or a JPEG graphic is like a mosaic made up of lots of pixels (tiny, single-colored squares). These are different from the "vector" graphics generated by drawing programs such as Freehand or Illustrator.

If you have been using pixel-based images in print design, such as TIFF, you are familiar with the term "resolution," or how many pixels per inch a graphic contains. For print, an image typically has a resolution of 300 dots per inch (or dpi).

On the Web, images need to be created at much lower resolutions. 72 dpi has become the *de facto* standard, but in reality, the whole notion of "inches" and even "dots per inch" becomes irrelevant in the Web environment. In the end, the only meaningful measurement is in actual number of pixels. Here's why.

Remember the nature of the Web: "you never know how your graphic will end up being displayed." When a graphic is displayed on a Web page, the pixels in the image map one-to-one with the display resolution of the monitor, and monitor resolution varies by platform. Allow me to demonstrate.

I have created a graphic that is 72 pixels square. Since I set the resolution to be 72 dots per inch, I expect that graphic to appear about one inch square when I view it on my monitor. And sure enough, since Macs tend to drive their monitors at a resolution of 72 dpi, it does appear to be about an inch square when I see it on my screen (Figure 6-3).

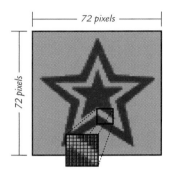

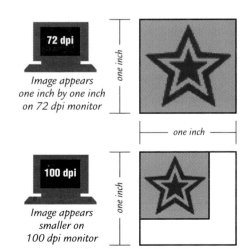

Image appears
one inch by one inch
on 72 dpi monitor

Image appears
smaller on
100 dpi monitor

But what happens when that same graphic is displayed on another platform? PC monitors tend to display at 96 dots per inch, and UNIX workstations and terminals drive their monitors at a resolution of 100+ pixels per inch. Let's take a look at my "one inch" graphic on a UNIX machine (Figure 6-3).

Suddenly, my inch-square graphic is less than a three-quarter inch square because those same 72 pixels are mapping one-to-one across 100 pixels per inch. For this reason, it is useless to think in terms of "inches" for the Web. And without inches, the whole notion of dots per inch is basically thrown out the window as well. The only thing we know for sure about the graphic is that it is 72 pixels across, and that it will be half the width of a graphic that is 144 pixels across.

After this example, it may also be clear now why this graphic would be a failure once it hits the Web if it were created at 300 dpi. Although it would still appear to be one inch wide in the graphics program I created it in, once it hits the one-to-one mapping method used by browsers, it could end up somewhere between three and four inches wide.

Despite the fact that a specific resolution is irrelevant, I consistently create my graphics at 72 dpi. Why? Because it at least gets me in the ballpark of appropriate resolutions for Web presentation. Also, I generate all of my graphics on a Mac, and my applications seem to work most comfortably and fonts render more smoothly in that 72 dpi groove.

Just know that if you're designing on a Mac with a standard monitor, most Internet users will be seeing your graphics smaller than you've designed them (Figure 6-4). If you can, check your work on a UNIX workstation for what is probably the worst case scenario.

Image size

Many people ask me how many inches across to make their graphics so that they will fit neatly into the browser window. The answer is related to many of the issues I've just discussed.

First, I've shown how inches aren't very useful online, so it's best to do your measuring in pixels. But even in pixels, there's no real way to know. Each browser over

FIGURE 6-4 ▶
*The same page viewed on Netscape on a Mac
vs. UNIX terminal.*

Mac terminal

UNIX terminal

each platform has a different default window width. In addition, we never know exaclty how wide each individual user has set his or her window.

For that reason, you can only guess. Most of the designers I know create full-width mastheads somewhere between 475 and 525 pixels. Remember, what doesn't fit in your Mac browser may actually have plenty of room left over in a Windows browser. And even if it doesn't fit exactly, users have the ability to re-size the window to make sure they aren't missing anything. You may choose to suggest an ideal window width either in text or by providing a graphic as a guideline.

The important thing is that you establish a scale for your site and then use it consistently.

creating graphics

E NOW KNOW THAT FILES on the Web need to end up as GIF files, and we've seen a few steps it takes to get them that way. But where do they begin? Where do these graphics come from?

Sometimes, you just need to start from scratch. This chapter will take a look at some methods for gathering images and setting text. We'll explore techniques for using both Adobe Photoshop and vector drawing programs as starting points for Web graphics creation. If you already have a graphic, but it's in the wrong format, we'll look at some ways to convert it to the necessary GIF format. Along the way, I hope to provide useful tips on production that might prevent problems from occurring down the road.

■ FINDING THE PICTURES

My guess is that you're going to want pictures somewhere on your Web page, right? Acquiring images to use in Web graphics is much the same as finding them for print, with a few extra considerations. Let's look at some possible sources for artwork that will make your page sing.

Electronic illustration

You might start with a drawing that has never seen paper. Since I enjoy illustrating, I often create my own images in a drawing program using a drawing tablet and stylus. Fractal Painter is an excellent pixel-based application for creating painterly illustrations and modifying photographs. You can open Painter files in Photoshop to add text and

I recommend scanning all black and white images in grayscale (8-bit), not in bitmap (2-bit) mode. This enables you to make adjustments in the midtone areas once you have sized the image to its final presentation dimensions and resolution.

In general, I prefer to scan both color and black and white images at a resolution of at least 144 dpi, so I can resize, adjust colors/contrast, etc., with somewhat more control.

additional effects. Sometimes I'll even use Photoshop to do small illustrations, though that is not what it was primarily designed to do.

Scanning

Scanning is a great way to collect source material for Web graphics. You can scan almost anything, from flat art to actual 3-D objects. Beware, however, the temptation to scan and use existing images. Keep in mind that most images you find are probably copyright-protected and may not be used without permission, unless the use is solely editorial. Never assume that you can use an existing image, even if you modify it considerably. Remember that millions of people have access to the World Wide Web (that's the "world wide" part), and using images for which you do not have permission can put you and your client at risk.

PhotoCDs or clip art disks

Once again, don't be seduced by some of the images you may come across on PhotoCD catalogs of stock images. If you haven't bought the rights to use the images, you just can't use them. And read the license carefully before you do buy any collections of images or clip art; some require additional payment for use of those images on the Internet. That said, PhotoCD and clip art collections are just wonderful resources for graphics.

Clip art is usually in vector format, created in applications like Freehand or Illustrator, and you can assign any size and resolution when you open the file into Photoshop. If the clip art files are EPS files that won't open in Photoshop, use a conversion utility such as EPS Converter to create a file that will open in Photoshop.

■ WORKING WITH TYPE

You can create text in your graphics either directly in Adobe Photoshop or by importing Freehand or Illustrator files. Either method works well, though you will get different results, depending on the typeface and size. Experiment with your typeface to see which method gives you the best results.

If you are using a typeface that you need to extend, compress, or set on a curve,

■ PHOTOCD TIPS

PhotoCD collections generally include four or five versions of each image at different resolutions. If I am pulling an image off of a PhotoCD, I generally start with a 144 or 150 dpi resolution version of the image and then resize it after I've done any masking or other image manipulation. If I know that there will also be a need for a print version of my work, I always use the high resolution version of any file from a PhotoCD.

I recommend creating the text in Freehand or Illustrator first, because they both have more exacting methods than Photoshop for manipulating text.

For small text, use relatively bold weights of sans serif fonts, such as Helvetica, Helvetica Condensed, Futura, Futura Condensed, and Stone Sans, to name just a few.

If you create a logotype for print that may be used on the Web, be sure to consider how it will look on screen at a reduced size and at 72 dpi. Fonts with lots of delicate detail quickly lose their crispness and legibility.

■ CREATING GRAPHICS IN ADOBE PHOTOSHOP

Now that we've discussed some of the origins of images and type, it's time to put them all together and save them in the Web's favorite flavor—GIF. And there's no application better suited for the task than Adobe Photoshop 3.0. In this section, we'll take a look at creating GIF files from a number of different starting points.

To convert a file to GIF format, you first have to ensure that the file uses 256 colors or fewer. As mentioned briefly on page 62, Photoshop has a mode called "Indexed Color." Indexed Color images use a color table containing between 2 and 256 colors. In Photoshop, when you change an RGB image to Indexed Color, you are building a color table for the image. The color table contains the colors that are used in the document. An RGB image may have millions of colors, but an indexed color image can only contain up to 256 colors. If a color in the RGB image is not present in the color table, Photoshop matches the color to the closest color in the table or simulates the color using several of the available colors with a diffusion filter.

From RGB to Indexed Color

To save an RGB image as a GIF file, you first have to convert it to Indexed Color. In Photoshop, the process is simple. First, if you have created a layered document, save it as the master file. I usually give it the suffix ".psd" to make clear that it is my layered Photoshop file. Then, select Mode and Indexed Color. Dialog boxes will appear asking you four questions: whether you want to flatten the layers (you do); what bit resolution you want to convert it to; what color palette to use; and what dithering method to use. (See the figure on page 33 in Chapter 3.)

■ BIT DEPTH

"Bit depth" is a way to refer to the maximum number of colors a graphic can contain. It is based on the storage of binary information (values described in ones and zeros). I think of each "bit" as a slot for a one or a zero. If a graphic has a bit depth of n, the maximum number of colors it can represent is 2^n. If you don't have a calculator handy, you can use this little chart:

1-bit:	2 colors
2-bit:	4 colors
3-bit:	8 colors
4-bit:	16 colors
5-bit:	32 colors
6-bit:	64 colors
7-bit:	128 colors
8-bit:	256 colors
24-bit:	16,777,216 *(usually just referred to as "millions" of colors)*

Bit resolution (bit depth)

You can select the number of colors you'd like to appear in the image by setting the bit resolution (bit depth) for the image, from three bits to eight bits. You may also choose "Other" and enter a specific number of colors between 2 and 256. The bit resolution you select determines how many colors will be allotted to the image. See the sidebar on this page for more information on bit depth.

Color palettes

There are five different palette options in Photoshop for the Macintosh for Indexed Color images (these options may be different for Photoshop running on a PC). Each has its own characteristics, and results in a different line-up of colors in the Color Table (available under "Mode" after you've converted to Indexed Color).

Exact Palette uses the palette that already exists in the RGB image, if the RGB image uses 256 colors or fewer. When you select this option, there is no dithering. This option will not work if there are more than 256 colors in the RGB image.

System Palette uses the Macintosh's default color table, which is based on a uniform sampling of RGB colors. If the bit depth selected is less than 8-bit, this option is labeled *Uniform*. You will also be asked to select a dithering option (see next page).

Adaptive Palette creates a color table that uses colors from the RGB image. Photoshop samples the entire image (or a selected area of the image) and chooses the colors that are most commonly used. If you select an area of the image, Photoshop will modify the sampling of the entire image to include more information from the selected area in the final color table.

Custom Palette allows you to create your own color table. When you select this option, the program displays the color table dialog box. You can then edit the colors that appear in the table and save the custom table you have created for later use. See the Photoshop User Manual for specific information on creating custom color palettes.

Previous Palette is only available once you've done a conversion with either the Adaptive or Custom option selected. Previous Palette uses the last previously used Custom palette.

Dithering options

Dithering is used to create the illusion that there are more colors in an image than really exist in the color table. Dithering mixes the pixels of the available colors to simulate additional colors. There are three dithering options:

None turns dithering off. The color closest to the missing color is used. This choice can make for very sharp edges between shades of color in an image.

Pattern, which is only available if you select the System Palette, creates patterns of random pixels to simulate colors not in the color table.

Diffusion creates a pattern of random pixels to simulate colors not in the color table. Diffusion may be used with the Adaptive, Custom, System, or Previous Palette options. The diffusion method of creating random pixels is less structured than that of the Pattern dithering option.

Once you have made your selections, Photoshop will convert the file to Indexed Color. Then you can save it as a GIF file.

NOTE: Although you may create a 4-bit color table for an image, Adobe Photoshop still treats the document as an 8-bit image. So, don't think that the file size number in the lower left corner of your Photoshop image window is the actual file size of your final file. That file size number refers to what Photoshop sees and displays, which is always an 8-bit image, even though the actual file size on your hard drive may be considerably smaller. To find a more accurate file size indicator, select the file on the desktop and choose "Get Info" from the menu.*

From grayscale to Indexed Color

To save a grayscale image as a GIF file, you first have to convert it from grayscale to Indexed Color. Open the grayscale image, select Mode and change the mode to Indexed Color. You will not be asked about your desired bit depth, color palette, or the diffusion method, because the computer has exactly 256 levels of gray available. If you want to set the number of pixel colors to fewer than 256 (and you probably will), you need to change the Mode to RGB first, and then to Indexed Color. If you skip that step, it will automatically save it as an 8-bit grayscale image.

* This file size represents not just the data that makes up the image, but also Macintosh-specified resource information that is tacked on. When you use a file transfer utility such as Fetch to send the file to a server as "raw data," the resource part of the file is stripped out, leaving it even smaller than it appears in the "Get Info" window. For a more specific file size report, you can use a shareware utility such as Snitch, which gives a precise breakdown of the data and resource information. I find it useful when I'm trying to target a specific file size. You can download Snitch at *http://hyperarchive.lcs. mit.edu/HyperArchive.html* (search for "snitch").

1. In Adobe Photoshop, change the mode from bitmap to grayscale.

2. Using the Image Size option, change the dimensions and the resolution (which should be 72 dpi).

3. The resulting image may look a bit fuzzy, and there may be midtone areas created by the size reduction that are a bit too dark or too light.

   If the image is too dark or too light in midtone areas, use the Adjust Image Curves option to pull the midtones lighter or darker.

   If the image is a bit fuzzy, use the Unsharp Mask filter (under Sharpen in the Filters menu) to sharpen the focus.

4. You can leave the image in grayscale, if you have enough room in your color map to accommodate the additional grays it uses, or else convert it back to a bitmap (two colors). Experiment with different threshold levels to see what looks best. In general, I prefer to keep the image as a grayscale image, even though this may mean slightly longer download times. It just looks better.

From bitmap (black and white) to Indexed Color

Unfortunately, if you are starting with a bitmap image (either scanned or from a CD), there's no way to change the mode directly to Indexed Color. You can change the mode from bitmap to grayscale and then directly to Indexed Color, but as noted above, the color table will contain 256 shades of gray. If you want the file to be black and white only, change from bitmap to grayscale to RGB, and then to Indexed Color so you have the chance to specify the number of "colors," in this case just two: black and white. The GIF file with only two colors will be smaller than the version with 256, and file size is always a consideration on the Web.

Changing the size and resolution of images

If you need to resize a graphic, whether by changing dimensions or by lowering its resolution, be sure to first change the mode to one that allows you the most pixel colors to play with. This way, when the application changes the resolution, it has a greater color or tonal range to draw from as it selects pixels to redraw the image at the new size.

For color images, working in RGB mode allows Photoshop millions of shades to choose from. If you are creating a graphic in RGB mode, be sure to do any resizing *before* converting it to Indexed Color.

Similarly, if you need to change the size of an existing GIF image for use on a Web page, convert the GIF to RGB color before you change the image size. Use the Unsharp Mask filter to sharpen things up before you convert the image back to Indexed Color to be saved as a GIF file. (Remember, don't copy and reuse GIF images you come across in your travels on the Web. Those images are probably protected by copyright law.)

When resizing a bitmap, first change it to a grayscale image. The resulting image, though it started as a high contrast image, will become a continuous tone image once the resolution has been reduced. See the *Resizing Bitmap Files* sidebar for details on the process.

■ STARTING FROM SCRATCH WITH FREEHAND OR ILLUSTRATOR

Although Photoshop is a primary tool for creating Web graphics, you can also create your graphics in applications like Adobe Illustrator or Macromedia Freehand.

These applications are *vector*, or object-based, programs that use mathematically-defined lines and curves to create shapes. When you create a graphic in a vector program, you are creating a geometric form that is scalable without loss of image quality or edge sharpness. Fractal Painter and Adobe Photoshop are *raster* programs, which are pixel-based. Raster-based applications create the actual pixels that make up an image. Although you can rescale raster images, the image quality and edge sharpness degrade when you rescale. Use vector-based applications to create things like logos, which will have to be used in both print and online materials. The scalability of vector graphics will enable you to resize your artwork for various uses, and you can convert the vector graphics to pixel graphics for use on the Web.

The Web requires the use of pixel-based graphics. In order to turn your vector graphics into the raster formats required for display via the Web, you will need to bring those graphics into a program like Photoshop or Debabelizer. Adobe Illustrator files will open into Photoshop directly; be sure to change any letterforms to paths before you save your Illustrator file. You can also open Freehand files, if properly saved, in Photoshop. For Freehand 5.0 and higher, you can export any Freehand file (or layers within a file) as a "Photoshop EPS" file, which can then be opened in Photoshop.

■ CONVERTING OTHER GRAPHICS FORMATS TO GIF

There are many different programs available that will convert from various graphics formats to GIF. Some programs give you greater control over the conversion method from an RGB to a 256-color (or fewer) image. Most conversion programs use proprietary algorithms for reducing millions of colors to 256 or fewer. You might want to test some of these programs to see which algorithms work best for your images. The combinations of variables (color tables, dithering options, etc.) are nearly endless.

Adobe Photoshop

For most designers, Photoshop will serve as the main conversion tool. Adobe Photoshop is an excellent conversion program. Photoshop can convert TIFF, EPS, PICT, BMP, PixelPaint, MacPaint, Targa, PIXAR, Amiga IFF, and JPEG files to GIF. For some

EPS files, such as those created in QuarkXpress or earlier versions of Freehand, you may need to run an EPS conversion program.

There is an excellent and inexpensive shareware application called EPS Converter, from Artemis Software, that will convert Quark and Freehand EPS files into files that will open in Photoshop. I often create complex text-heavy imagemap sketches in Quark and export them to Photoshop as templates for creating the actual graphics.

Using EPS Converter is simple: you just launch EPS Converter and then open the EPS file you wish to convert. It does the conversion and saves the file as an Illustrator file (with an *.art* file name), which can then be opened in Photoshop. The latest version of EPS Converter is available at *ftp://mac.archive.umich.edu/mac/graphics/graphicsutil/ epsconverter.*

Equilibrium Debabelizer and Debabelizer Lite

Debabelizer is a very powerful conversion tool if you're working on a Mac (sorry, no Windows version available). The application can open and convert over sixty different format types. There are all sorts of options for reducing the colors in an image and batch processing of images, which will be useful for anyone who has lots of images to convert. There are two versions of the program, Debabelizer and Debabelizer Lite. Debabelizer is commercial software, available at software stores and through mail-order catalogs.

Hijaak Pro and Hijaak 95 (Quarterdeck Software)

Quarterdeck Software has a couple of great tools for image conversion for Windows and Windows 95. Hijaak Pro is part of the Hijaak Graphics Suite, an integrated set of graphics utilities for Windows. Hijaak 95 is a Windows 95 conversion and image manipulation tool. Both applications can open and convert over 50 image format types. Like Debabelizer for the Macintosh, they include options for reducing the number of colors in an image in either manual or batch mode. They both also allow the user to adjust the contrast, gamma, and brightness of an image and resize it as well. Both applications are commercially available.

Shareware programs for the Mac

There are some excellent shareware programs for file conversion available via the Internet. The best of these are a great buy: inexpensive and very powerful. You can download them, try them out, and then pay the shareware fee. It's an honor system for the most part, so be sure to pay the fees for any shareware you keep and use on a regular basis. Many conversion shareware and freeware programs are available on the Web (and more are being developed every day), but here a few of my favorites:

- *GIFConverter* is a shareware program that can convert TIFF, RIFF, PICT, JPEG, MacPaint, and Thunderscan files to GIFs. GIFConverter can open and read several graphic file formats, including GIF, TIFF, RIFF, PICT, JPEG (JFIF), MacPaint, and Thunderscan. It can write these formats, as well as black-and-white EPS. It also prints on almost any Macintosh printer. You can use GIFConverter to convert files you find online for use in other programs, to view files, or to print them out.

  To use GIFConverter, double-click the GIFConverter icon, then open the file you want by choosing the Open command from the FIle menu. To convert to a different format, choose Save As... from the File menu, and select the format you want in the popup menu.

  Official releases and upgrades of GIFConverter can be downloaded from CompuServe at the Graphics Support Forum (GO GRAPHSUPPORT), library 3, the Macintosh RoundTable on GEnie, or from America Online in the Direct Connect folder of the Macintosh Graphics and CAD forum (keyword: mgr). GIFConverter updates are also available through some user groups, disk services, and Internet FTP sites.

- *GraphicConverter* imports almost every graphic file format you name, and can convert them all to GIF. It has a lot of options for converting RGB files to 8-bit color images and manipulating color tables. It also has some limited image manipulation capabilities.

  Using GraphicConverter is very straightforward. It comes with complete documentation if you want to explore its capabilities. For quick conversions, just launch the application and open your graphics file. Select Colors from the Picture menu and change the bit depth. (You can also change the resolution, or the proportions, or the scale of the image. All of these options are under the Picture menu.) Then save the file as a GIF. There is even an option in the Colors menu for setting a transparent background color in your GIF file.

GraphicConverter can convert complete folders or a set of pictures from one format to another format. You can find GraphicConverter on various Mac archives on the Internet (see page 102 in Chapter 9 for details) and on CompuServe (GO SWREG ! GraphicConverter is ID #1634). Don't forget to pay the registration fee if you find that you use GraphicConverter on a regular basis.

Shareware for Windows and Windows 95

Graphic Workshop for Windows is a well-written shareware program that displays, converts, and manipulates most image format types. You can download the software at *http://www.north.net/alchemy/* or ftp it from *ftp.north.net/pub/alchemy*.

■ A FEW TIPS ON PRODUCTION

Save! Save! Save!

Just as you would for any other desktop design, it is a good idea to save often and to save several versions of your work along the way. If you are creating your graphic in a layered Photoshop file, be sure to save the layered version separately from the "flattened" GIF file. It is much easier to make those inevitable changes to the layered file.

The name game

Be sure to use the proper file extension names for your graphics files. All GIF files use the format *filename.gif*. And keep your filenames as economical as possible: pre-Windows 95 versions of Windows software allow only 8 characters for the filename and 3 characters for the extension.

Resolving resolution

As a general rule, I work in 72 dpi at the final desired image dimensions when I am creating graphics from scratch for use on the Web. However, when I will need those same images at 300 dpi resolution (or higher) for print or slides, I take one of two approaches: I create the original art at 300 dpi (or the final high resolution dpi), save that version, and then resize it to 72 dpi and convert it to GIF format; or I create two versions of the artwork from scratch, one at 300 dpi and one at 72 dpi. There is no rule about which approach to take when having to produce one image at two very different resolutions—it all depends on the image characteristics—but start by making the 300 dpi version first, and then see what happens when you reduce it to 72 dpi. Once reduced, if it is unacceptable, try recreating the image from scratch at 72 dpi. Remember to always do the reduction (in RGB or grayscale) before you convert the file to Indexed Color, so as to get the best possible image quality at 72 dpi.

eight creating better graphics

SHOULD PROBABLY FIRST EXPLAIN what I mean by the word "better" in this chapter's title. I'm not going to tell you to use a certain font that makes your graphics more sophisticated or to introduce some special blur effect that will make your graphics decidedly more hip. By "better," I simply mean better optimized for the Web medium.

In my opinion, "good" Web graphics are those that are designed with sensitivity to a couple of Web-specific issues. The first, and most important, is the download time constraint that I covered earlier. The other factor to keep in mind is that graphics will be viewed on monitors of varying sophistication, from large 24-bit color monitors, down to the monochrome LCD displays on some laptop computers.

In this chapter, I'd like to show you some ways to create your graphics with the goal of improving your readers' Web-page viewing experience.

■ LIMITING FILE SIZE

At the risk of sounding like a broken record I'll say it one more time, "KEEP THOSE FILES SMALL!," or at least as small as possible without sacrificing too much quality. Just how much quality you want to sacrifice for download time is up to you. I tend to favor performance (i.e. quick download times) over pizazz.

But just how small is "small"? There are no hard and fast rules; in fact, I'm not sure there is even a general consensus, but I'll give you some numbers I've always used as a guideline.

Using the formula from page 48 (download time = 2 seconds per graphic + 1 second per K), a 30K graphic would take roughly 32 seconds to download under average conditions.*

Personally, I've decided that I don't want anyone waiting in front of a blank screen for more than 30 seconds or so, so I've specified 30K to be the *maximum* size for any graphic on the pages I design. Whenever possible, I strive to hit the 10K mark. My technical director recommends that a "graphics-lite" Web page would consist of 30K *total*—including the HTML file and all the inline graphics for that page. It's tight, but it can be done.

Granted, not everyone is following such stringent guidelines. I've come across inline graphics over 100K in size. You'll need to decide how important large, lush graphics are to the effectiveness of your site. If your intent is to create a visually rich online experience, then maybe it's worth the extra K. As a general rule, smaller is better regardless of what you're trying to accomplish with your site. Here are a couple of strategies for keeping file sizes in check.

Limit the dimensions of the graphic

Though fairly obvious, the easiest and most predictable way to keep file size down is to limit the dimensions of the graphic. There aren't any magic numbers; just don't make graphics larger than they need to be.

By eliminating a lot of extra white space and reducing the dimensions of my Tea Tin banner, I was able to reduce the file size by 5K (Figure 8-1). This is one of the ways I've tailored my design style to make it more appropriate to the Web.

As long as we're speaking about graphics' dimensions, I should mention that I am usually more concerned with the vertical measurement of a graphic than the horizontal. One reason is that when a Web page is viewed on a 14" monitor, there isn't much vertical real-estate. Limiting the height of the graphics allows more material to fit into a "screen-full."

Also, in HTML 2.0, images are always positioned flush left and there is no way to wrap text next to them. The best you get is one line of text, usually flush with the bottom of the image, and the rest is vast, wasted space. Limiting the height of graphics also limits all that white space on browsers that don't support the text-wrap tag. As a result, the graphics I create for the Web tend to be horizontally oriented.

*Many factors can skew this figure drastically one way or the other, such as the type of server, the machine the reader is using, and the amount of traffic over the lines. Consider this number as only the most basic, proportional measurement.

FIGURE 8-1 ▶

File size savings by cropping the image size

13K

8K

Limit the number of colors

Limiting the number of pixel colors can have a drastic effect on the file size of your graphic. GIF files can contain up to 8-bit color (256 pixel colors), but most often, you can render the image reasonably at a lower bit-depth.

At a certain point, of course, if you reduce the number of colors too far, the image will begin to fall apart or will cease to communicate the effect you are after. This "melt-down" point is different for different types of images.

Let's take a look at some examples to see how limiting the color affects file size of the final GIF. I've also included a JPEG version of the same image for comparison. In addition to watching the size, we'll be paying attention to the point at which the image quality becomes unacceptable.*

I've selected images that represent a range of image types. Image A, the Café scene, is an example of a full-color image made up of lots of shapes and colors, including flesh tones. Image B, the field of flowers, is another photographic image, but the palette is reduced to primarily yellow, green, and purple. Image C, a banner graphic for "Flowers, Incorporated," contains large areas of flat color. Image D, the green leaves, is a photographic image, but is almost totally monochromatic.

*Bear in mind throughout this exercise that just as online graphics can be a poor representation of print, so printed graphics can be a poor representation of graphics displayed on a monitor. Quality assessments will refer to how these graphics render on screen. You'll just have to trust me if it seems to contradict what appears on these pages.

Bit-depth and file size

◼ IMAGE A: THE CAFÉ SCENE

Not surprisingly, the 8-bit version starts off *huge*, and already, we can see some loss of subtle shades of color, such as the purple tint to the bag on the bicycle. By the 6-bit version, the flesh tones are getting kind of funky.

It isn't until we get down to the 4-bit version that the file size becomes reasonable for use as an inline image (using my totally made-up guideline of 30K). Unfortunately, by that time, there aren't enough pixel colors to render the image, and the quality is unacceptable. If this image absolutely had to appear inline, I would accept a slightly larger file size in order to retain some of the original flavor of the photo. Or I could opt to use the JPEG format inline and figure some users will just miss out.

8-Bit 69K

7-Bit 56K

6-Bit 46K

5-Bit 38K

JPEG 25K

4-Bit 31K

3-Bit 23K

IMAGE B: THE FIELD O' FLOWERS

Notice how the quality of this image holds up much better at lower bit-depths.

For this image, I think that even at 5-bit color (that's only thirty-two pixel colors) the photograph still conveys its original flavor. If the purpose of this graphic were to display a photographer's work, then of course, the highest quality would have to be maintained. But if it's just for decoration, 5-bit would be fine with me.

Notice that the file size is larger than my 30K limit, but sometimes you need to compromise for the sake of quality. As the designer, you decide where to draw the line.

8-Bit 81K

7-Bit 68K

6-Bit 52K

5-Bit 43K

JPEG 26K

4-Bit 33K

3-Bit 24K

■ IMAGE C: THE FLOWERS, INC. LOGO

You should notice right away that the file sizes for this image are drastically lower, even though the dimensions are the same as the previous examples. This difference is due to the wide areas of flat color that the GIF compression scheme can condense more than photographic images.

You may also notice that the savings in file size in the JPEG version isn't as great as it was for the previous examples. Although JPEG is much better at compressing photographic images, GIF is actually a little more efficient at handling flat graphics.

8-Bit 30K

7-Bit 26K

6-Bit 18K

5-Bit 14K

JPEG 13K

4-Bit 11K

3-Bit 9K

■ IMAGE D: GREEN LEAVES

I had originally thought that this image would demonstrate that a limited color palette would lead to a smaller file size. Boy, was I surprised when this turned out to be the largest one of all!

When I looked at it again, I realized that although virtually everything in the image is green, every surface is shaded with gradated tones. There really aren't any areas of flat color for the GIF compression to squeeze down.

Interestingly, this image remains fairly well-rendered even at 3-bit color depth (that's only eight pixel colors).

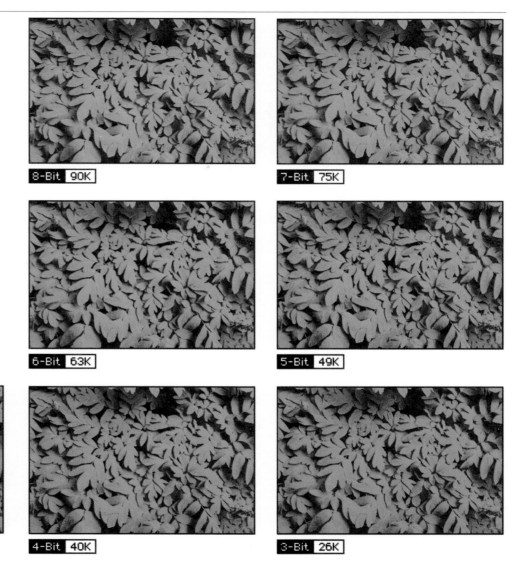

As we've seen in the examples, limiting the number of pixel colors in your image can certainly reduce the size of your graphic. One of the things I've found most interesting is how far a few pixels can go! I limit nearly all of the graphics in my Web pages to 5-bit colors (32 colors). I'll use 4-bit color (16 colors) whenever possible, especially for graphics that are made up of mainly text. I reserve 6-bit color depth for special occasions, such as when I need the extra colors to prevent a flesh tone from turning green. (I might point out here that although I usually work in even bit-depths, it is possible to specify an exact number of pixel colors somewhere between the even bit depth limits.)

As usual, I recommend testing. I usually start low, choosing 4-bit in the Indexed Color dialog box, then deciding whether I can live with it. If the image falls apart or just looks unaccepably yucky, I'll "undo" and try it again with more pixel colors. Eventually, by inching up the pixel count, I arrive at an image I can live with.

Design with flat areas of color

Another useful lesson to be gained from the example images is that images with flat areas of color will condense down much further. I've found it useful to know a little bit about how GIF compression works. Note, this isn't technically accurate, but will give you a basic visual model of the process.

The GIF compression scheme condenses rows of pixels. When it hits a long string of pixels of the same color, it can save this information in a single description.

description = "15 blue"

In an image with gradations of color, it has to store a description for every pixel in the row. The longer description means a larger file size.

description = "1 blue", "1 aqua", "1 lighter aqua", ...

JPEG file at best quality—64K

JPEG file at medium quality—25K

JPEG file at low quality—18K

Reducing the number of pixel colors in an image (as demonstrated above) is, in effect, just a way of creating more flat-color areas by combining similar, abutting pixels. But you can help the process even further by just designing your Web graphics with a lot of flat color areas right off the bat.

I stay away from effects like gradated fills for my online work. In most cases, they aren't absolutely necessary, and it's the first sort of thing I'd sacrifice for the cause of quicker download times.

If I have a great photographic image that complements a headline, I try to reduce its dimensions and make it a *part* of the graphic, instead of filling the whole thing. I've followed this strategy for the Flowers, Inc. logo example. That banner might have also been nice with a completely flowered background with the type reversed out. But since I knew I was designing the graphic to go online, I used enough of the flower image for flavor, but used flat colors to fill the majority of the space.

You should be aware that if you've chosen "Dither" in Photoshop while converting to Indexed Color, the areas that you've filled with flat color may end up speckled with different colored pixels as a result of the dithering effect. You could decide to live with it, or, if you are earnest in your quest for the smallest file size possible, you could spend some time cleaning the area up. This process can be done a number of ways within Photoshop, including selecting the area and re-filling it while in Indexed Color mode or by dabbing at the stray pixels with the pencil tool. You'll need to decide whether it's worth the extra work.

Fine-tuning JPEG compression

If you are using JPEG graphics, whether external or inline, you have some options for how you'd like your graphic compressed. In Photoshop, when you save in the JPEG format, you get a dialog box that essentially asks you whether you value compression or quality. If you aren't sure how to answer, it's a good idea to run some tests to see which of the results is a good balance of acceptable file size and image quality.

Figure 8-2 shows some possible variations of JPEG compression and how the quality and file size are affected. In this example, image quality did not deteriorate noticeably even at the lowest quality compression.

■ WINDOWS PALETTE ON THE MAC

If you create your graphics in Adobe Photoshop for the Mac and are concerned about how they will look to Windows users, you can use colors from the Windows palette right from the start.

Start with any image that uses the Windows palette. If you have access to a Windows machine, just take a screen shot and save the image. Another method is to open a new file in Macromedia Director on your Mac and choose the Windows palette.

Once you've got your "Windows" graphic, open it in Photoshop, convert it to Indexed Color; choose "Custom" under the palette options, then save that palette so you can use it again later. I save palettes in the "Goodies" folder in the Photoshop folder.

Now that you've captured the Windows palette, you can "Load" it into the Swatches floating palette and choose the colors for your graphic from there. You can also apply the Windows palette to a graphic you've already created by loading it in the Color Table dialog box.

*The Gamma control panel comes with Adobe Photoshop 3.0 in the calibration folder.

■ COLOR ON THE WEB

As you might guess, color is another one of those things that goes a little haywire when it gets on the Web. Like fonts and page sizes, color has always been a part of my designs that I was accustomed to controlling (that's what a press check is for, right?). On the Web, as I've said before, you just don't know how it's going to be seen.

The key fact to remember is that Web pages are viewed on a seemingly endless variety of browsers, monitors, and operating systems. Each has its own way of handling the color information it encounters. Like so many other factors of Web design, although you can't know for sure how it's going to look, you can take some basic measures to improve the appearance of your graphics even in a low-end viewing environment.

Gamma settings

I think I'll introduce this topic by telling a little story about luscious graphics gone awry. One of my early designs for the original GNN interface was based on a rich, midnight blue that I used consistently throughout the site. I liked to think of this color as "GNN-blue." Then one day, I saw the same page displayed on a color UNIX terminal. To my surprise, GNN-blue was displaying as GNN-black! Not only that, the wonderfully intense deep greens, browns, and grays that I love to design with so much—black, black, and black.

The reason for the discrepancy is that I created these graphics on a Mac, and Macs tend to display colors much lighter than PCs or UNIX terminals. On my screen, I was able to see the subtlety of the dark shades, but all of that was lost when it appeared on other platforms. Likewise, graphics that are generated on a PC will look a little washed-out when they hit a Mac.

To compensate for this difference, I use a control panel called "Gamma,"* which alters the overall brightness of my monitor. Now, I keep the gamma set to 2.2, the darkest setting, in order to simulate a UNIX or PC viewing environment. That way, I know that even the darkest colors will be readable to the majority of viewers with color monitors.

I simply switch the gamma setting back to 1.4 for a quick check of how Mac users will see my graphics—a bit lighter, but usually OK. If I'm working under the darkest gamma setting and creating graphics with lots of subtle light shades, I can check to see that these colors aren't washing out to white.

System palettes

256 colors is 256 colors, right? Nope. One of my early lessons is that although Macs and PCs running Windows can both run monitors with a palette of 256 colors (8-bit), they are using different sets of 256. For this reason, colors that look smooth on my monitor, even if I have it set to 8-bit color, can look unattractively dithered when it's rendered in a Windows environment.

This issue also applies to browser background colors. I had chosen a nice shade of almond for the background of one of my Web pages, but when it loaded onto a PC, it created a dithered pattern that made it difficult to read the text. (For more information on how to set background colors, see pages 134–136 in Chapter 11.)

If you find the dithering of your graphics unacceptable, you can head the problem off at the pass by making sure the colors in your graphics are taken from the standard Windows color palette.

If you are using a Macintosh, check out the powerful graphics program called DeBabelizer, which can convert your Mac palette to the closest Windows equivalents. By doing this conversion, you have a chance to see how your graphics will look to the millions of PC users out there.

Note that this is not exactly catering to the "lowest common denominator." Be aware that many PCs and Macs have only sixteen available colors with which to render your graphics. The results can be pretty scary. I've made the decision to draw the line at 256 and just hope for the best for lesser displays. If you can't live with this, or if you know absolutely that your target audience was viewing the Web under these conditions, you might decide to use those same sixteen color palettes exclusively in your designs.

The Web in black and white

As long as we're talking about the lowest common denominator, let's think about the user who only sees the Web made up of black and white pixels. Granted, their experience won't be nearly as rich as in full-color, but for them, I try to make sure that my graphics are at least functional. By functional, I mean that they won't miss out on some crucial bit of information, such as the name of the company or a navigational cue, because the type in the graphic is illegible. If the crucial bit of information lies in the picture, then I do my best to make sure that the image can be made out through all the dithering.

Mac users can get an approximation of how their graphic will render on a monochrome monitor by simply changing the monitor control panel setting to black and white. I've even created a keyboard short-cut so I can toggle between black and white and 24-bit color quickly.

When a color image is displayed on a monochrome monitor, the result is a dithered image made up of black and white pixels that approximate the values in the image. I've found that high contrast images suffer less in the translation, so I try to keep my images as "contrasty" as possible, especially when dealing with type.

To make sure type will be readable even in black and white, I first choose a clean, simple font at a size that is substantial enough not to get lost in the dithering. Then I'll make sure that I place it against a background that is of contrasting value—a light background for dark type and vice versa (Figure 8-3). Sometimes I'll add a black drop shadow below the type to boost the contrast a little more (although, it also increases the number of pixel colors).

In the lower images in Figure 8-3, the delicate purple type is virtually lost against a teal background when viewed in black and white, because the type and background colors are so close in value. Be aware also, that for very small type the anti-aliasing (the softening of edges for a smoother effect) that makes the type much easier to read in color can make it nearly illegible in black and white. What can you do about it? Not much other than to continue to test until you get something you're happy with. After seeing enough test images, you'll develop a feel for what works and what doesn't.

Contrasty color example

Good in black and white

Low-contrast color example

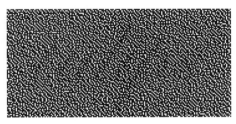

Bad in black and white

nine transparency and interlacing

TRANSPARENCY AND INTERLACING are nifty tricks you can only do with graphics in an online medium such as the Web. In this chapter I'll explain what these words mean and show you step-by-step how to create these effects in your graphics.

Before we get started, I'd like to say a word about tools. The methods in this chapter rely on special utilites or applications with which you might not be familiar. There are *lots* of tools out there that can perform these tasks, so I can't demonstrate all of them. Instead, I'll stick to what I consider to be the most popular or the easiest to use tools available as of this writing (giving a special edge to those that are available by downloading them right off the Net).

Again, I'm sticking to tools available for the Mac throughout this chapter. PC users should check out "The Transparent GIF Page" *(http://dragon.jpl.nasa.gov/~adam/ transparent.html)*. It includes information on the tools available for both transpareny and interlacing, as well as links to download them.

Allow me to get some gabbing out of the way before we go on to the nitty-gritty demonstrations.

■ TRANSPARENCY

All bitmapped graphics, such as GIF files, are rectangular by nature, but you can create the illusion that your graphic has a more interesting shape. You do this by setting portions of your graphic to be "transparent" so that the browser's background

FIGURE 9-1 ▶

The graphic on the left is not transparent. In the graphic on the right, the non-image areas have been made transparent, and the browser's background color show through.

color (or pattern, for that matter) will show through (see Figure 9-1). Transparency is one of my favorite tricks in Web design. I quickly got sick of every graphic being in a rectangle (it's not like that in other media), so it's nice to give them bumps, curves, or pointy things.

There is a special kind of GIF format, called "GIF89a," that can handle the extra information necessary for transparency. At this time, virtually all browsers can interpret the GIF89a format and support transparency, but that was not always the case. A few older versions of browsers may still be in use that won't display your graphics as transparent.

To create a transparent GIF, you must specify a pixel color that you'd like to be transparent, and then save the graphic as a GIF89a file. There is a shareware utility for the Mac called *Transparency* that does just that (and *only* that). For PC users, *GIFTrans* will perform the same task.

The demonstration of transparency techniques begins on page 96 of this chapter. In addition to the basics, I'll show you a few tricks for fine-tuning your transparent graphics.

■ INTERLACING

This effect is kind of hard to explain, but if you've spent any time looking at the Web, I know you've seen it. If a graphic is *not* interlaced, it displays in the browser either all at once (when the last bit of information is received) or one row of pixels at a time, from top to bottom, until the entire picture is complete. Over a good connection, this process may not even be perceptible. However if the graphic is very large over a

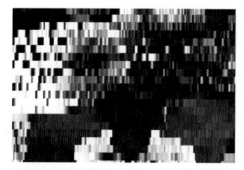

▲ FIGURE 9-2:
An interlaced GIF downloading

slow connection, you could wait a long time with a lot of empty screen while the data downloads. Without interlacing, the browser only displays the clear and final image.

Interlacing is a way to put a hint of the upcoming image on the screen while the rest of the data is downloading. The entire image area first fills in with what looks like a blurry mosaic. Then it gradually gets more and more defined as the data flows in (Figure 9-2). You end up waiting just as long for the clear image, but at least there's something happening while you wait.

To interlace or not to interlace

Whether you interlace your graphic is entirely your design decision. There's no reason why graphics must be created this way, and two schools of thought exist on their use. Many people (most of them designers, interestingly enough) would rather see nothing at all than have to look at a blurry mess on their screens. In addition, interlacing may actually cause your graphic to take longer to download.

The vast majority of folks seem to think that interlacing is indispensable and that you have to give users something to look at so they know what they are waiting for. If there is a link in that graphic, the user can click there before the image is fully downloaded (a time saver), and if they can make a quicker decision to go "back" if they arrived at the wrong place. Some people just say it looks cool.

So, the decision is yours. I'll show you some ways to make a graphic interlaced starting on page 102 in this chapter. See page 147 in Chapter 12, *More Web tricks*, for a nifty alternative to interlacing.

Making graphics transparent

 TOOLS: Transparency

The trick to transparency is that you're designating one pixel color to essentially become "invisible." Anything in the browser background (even a tiled graphic pattern) will show through these areas.

1. Open a GIF file in Transparency ("Open File" or drag file onto Transparency icon).

2. Position the eyedropper over the area you'd like to be transparent. Click and hold until the color panel appears. Each field in the panel corresponds to a pixel color in your image (the same as the Indexed Color table in Photoshop). You can also drag the dropper around in the color panel to choose a different pixel color.

3. When you let go of the mouse button, all the pixels in the image that are your selected color will turn gray. This gray area will be rendered as transparent when it is displayed in a browser.

4. In the File menu, choose "Save as GIF89a" (Command-S). You can replace it or rename the file.

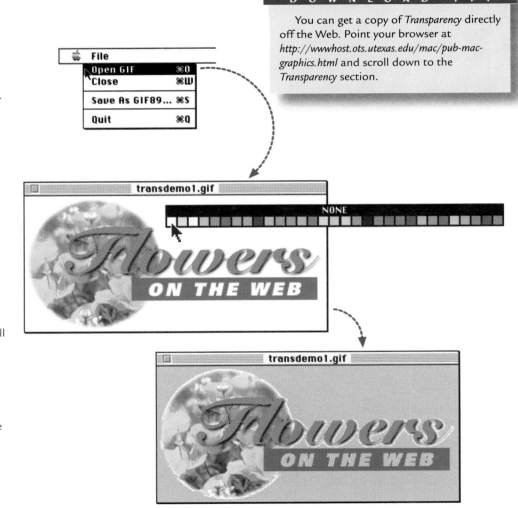

Transparency tips & tricks

TIP ONE: BETTER CONTROL OVER TRANSPARENT AREAS

TOOLS: Adobe Photoshop 3.0; Transparency

ote that all the pixels of that color appearing in the graphic will turn transparent. As you can see below, when I specified that I'd like the white border of my graphic to be transparent, my white type went transparent as well!

Netscape: GIF image 390x181 pixels

I nearly always use white for the areas that I'd like to turn transparent.* Obviously, I create lots of images that have white pixels in them that I'd like to remain white, such as the white type in the above example. To do this, I create a second white in the Indexed Color Table. The first one stays white, and the second one can be set to transparent.

Even if white isn't your color of choice, you can follow the same steps and specify some other color. Regardless of the color you choose, the following technique is still a useful way to ensure that no pixels within your image area will turn transparent.

*At one time, I was told that most browsers that did not support the GIF89a format were programmed with white as their default background color. If the "transparent" areas of my graphic were white, it would just blend into the white browser background and still give the illusion of transparency (another example of keeping the lowest common denominator in mind).

1. Open your GIF file in Photoshop (or change mode to Indexed Color if graphic isn't saved in GIF format yet).

2. Using the magic wand tool, with anti-aliasing turned OFF (very important!), select all the areas you intend to make transparent. I usually set the tolerance very low, between 8 and 24, so I don't grab too many pixels and break up delicate type or edges. Be sure to get all the little areas within characters such as "o" and "a."

   Warning: don't use "Select Similar" or you will select all the pixels of that color that appear in the image. The idea here is to just select the ones you intend to turn transparent later.

3. Fill that area with a new color that doesn't already appear in the image.

   a. Change Mode to RGB (this allows you to add a new color; in Indexed Color the number of colors is fixed).

   b. In the color selector, choose a bright, obnoxious color that you are certain doesn't appear anywhere in your image. I find the first five or six swatches in the default color selector work well for this.

   c. Fill the selected area with the bright color (option-delete).

   d. Check the picture to make sure all the little areas that should be transparent are filled with the bright color.

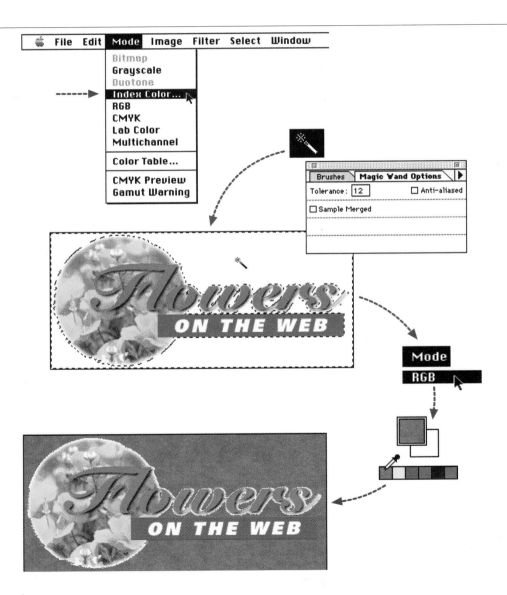

4. Change Mode back to Indexed Color (be sure it has the number of colors you want; adding the bright color may add one extra color).

5. Change that new bright color to white. This will be your second, or "new," white.

   a. Under Mode in menu, choose "Color Table."

   b. Click on the bright color (it should be easy to find). Make a mental note of where it appeared in the table.

   c. In the Color Palette Information panel, enter the following values to turn the selected color white: H=0, S=0, B=100 (the rest will adjust themselves).

   d. Hit "OK" to exit Color Palette; hit "OK" to exit Color Table.

   e. Your chosen area should turn white.

6. Save as CompuServe GIF.

7. When you open the new file in Transparency, be sure to choose the "new" white (it should appear in the same position in Transparency's color table as in Photoshop's indexed color chart).

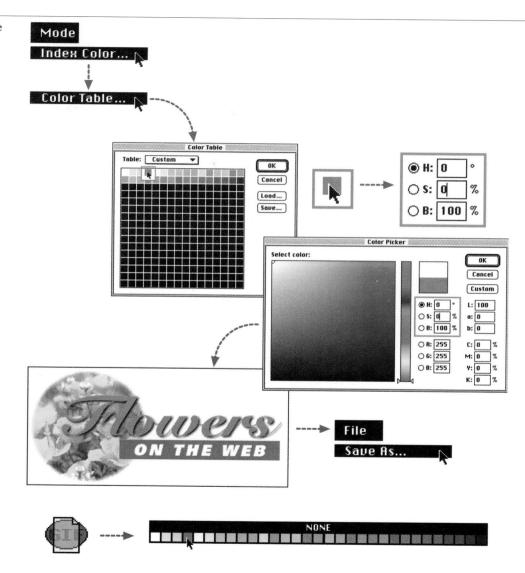

TIP TWO: AVOIDING "HALOS" AROUND TRANSPARENT GRAPHICS

  TOOLS: Adobe Photoshop 3.0; Transparency

Note: For this technique to work, you need to start with a layered Photoshop graphic. The parts of your graphic must be on transparent layers without any surrounding pixels. In other words, the image must not have already been "flattened."

If you are starting with a flattened image, such as a picture from a PhotoCD, you can select the area or object you'd like to appear in your graphic, then copy and paste it into a new layered Photoshop file with the background set to "Transparent." Make sure that the anti-aliasing feature of the selection tool is turned ON so the edges of your selection will be soft.

1. In Photoshop, while the graphic is still layered, create a new layer at the bottom of the "stack." In the example, this layer is named "background."

Now my white text stays white, even though the transparent areas are set to white as well. But take a look at all the light-colored pixels around the edge of the image. I call this a "halo," and it is the result of the anti-aliased pixels around the edge of the image. I find that it ruins the transparency effect. I like the transition from image to background to be smooth and seamless, without a lot of light-colored fringe. If you create your files according to the following technique, you should be able to prevent these halos from happening. The trick is to make sure those anti-aliased pixels are blending to a color that is close in color and value to the final background color of the Web page in the browser. The process begins in Photoshop 3.0.

Layered Image

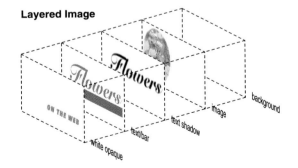

Flattened Image

2. Completely fill that layer with a color that is close to the final background color of your Web page. If it's impossible to match exactly, it's better to guess a little darker than the Web page shade.

   In my example, I assume that my page will be viewed against the browser's default light gray, so I've chosen a gray that is close to that. If you know that you are specifying a different background color for your page, then fill your bottom layer with that color.

3. When the visible layers are merged as a result of changing the Mode to Indexed Color, anti-aliased text and other soft edges will blend to the color of your bottom layer.

   By blending to a color that is close to (or even a little darker than) the target background color for the browser, you can be assured that no pixels along the edge will be lighter than the background. And thus, no halos!

4. At this point, just follow the instructions above for selecting areas for transparency.

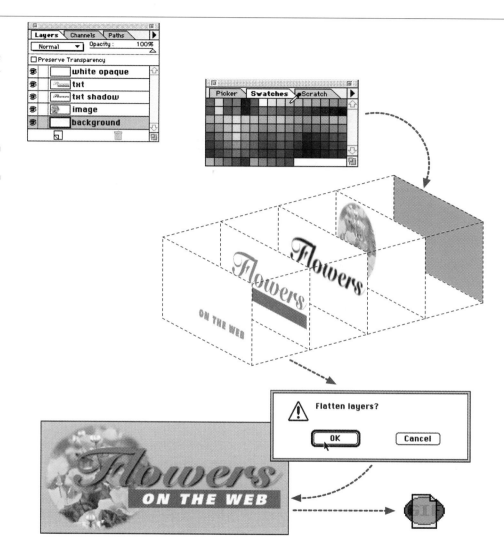

Interlacing graphics

  TOOLS: Adobe Photoshop 3.0; GIFConverter

Note: These steps will work for both GraphicConverter and GIFConverter. These programs have other functions and uses besides interlacing. Read the accompanying documentation for more information.

1. Open your GIF file in the program.

2. Choose "Save as..." from the file menu.

3. Click "OPTIONS," and select "Interlacing," then hit "OK."

Important: If you plan to make your graphic both interlaced and transparent using these tools, you need to make it interlaced first, and set the transparency last. You do this process because only the Transparency utility is capable of saving the graphic in GIF89a format.

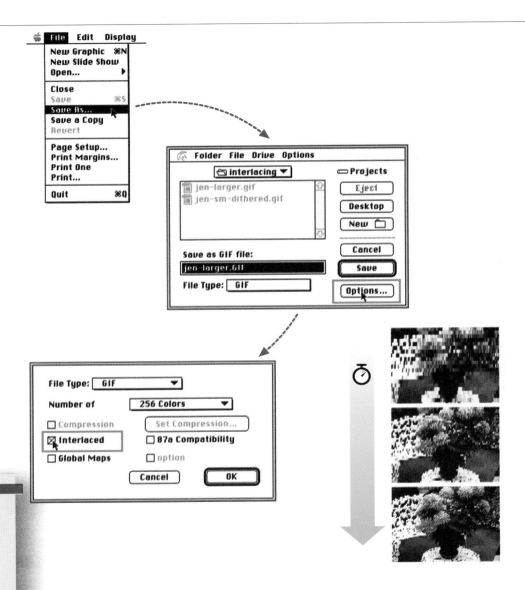

Using Photoshop plug-ins for transparency and interlacing

 TOOLS: Photoshop with the PhotoGIF & Adobe plug-ins

■ USING PHOTOGIF (A PHOTOSHOP PLUG-IN BY BOXTOP SOFTWARE)

With PhotoGIF, you just save your file in the PhotoGIF format, as opposed to the CompuServe GIF format that we've been using in previous demonstrations. For this reason, you should follow all previous instructions for preparing your graphic to be saved as a GIF.

1. Choose "Save as" from the File Menu. Give your file a name that ends with ".gif."

2. In that same dialog box, choose "Photo-GIF" from the list of available formats.

unning each and every graphic through lots of little utilities is a cumbersome process. Not surprisingly, major graphics applications are beginning to add Web-specific tools to their toolboxes.

Two plug-ins currently exist for Photoshop, one by Adobe (which only works with Version 3.0.5) and another by a third-party developer called BoxTop Software. They work slightly differently, but both give Photoshop the ability to save a graphic in the GIF89a format (thus enabling transparency) and to specify the interlacing function.

These products, and others like them, are under development and are likely to be enhanced by the time this book hits the shelves, but I felt I should include them here as hints of better tools to come. And I should note, these tools have functionality beyond what I describe here. You should read all the accompanying documentation to get the most out of the tools.

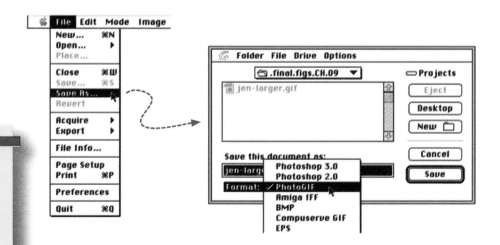

3. The PhotoGIF dialog box appears.

   a. You can turn interlacing on or off with the checkbox.

   b. If you want to turn an area transparent, select the "GIF89a" button. A color table will appear. Choose the color you'd like to be transparent by selecting the color from the table.

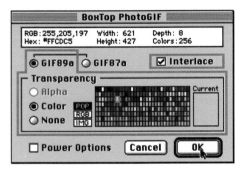

4. Select "Save" when you have everything set the way you want.

Note: Choosing a color from a table isn't as easy as using the eyedropper tool found in Transparency, but the folks at BoxTop promise an eyedropper tool in future releases of PhotoGIF. In the meantime, I find it easiest to select the pixel color from the table when the colors are arranged the same as they appear in Photoshop's color table (especially if I've created a "second white" as shown above). Choosing the "IMG" button will line up the colors in the "Photoshop" order.

■ USING ADOBE'S PLUG-IN

Adobe's plug-in saves graphics in the GIF89a format by exporting them rather than saving. Otherwise, the process is similar. After you've converted the image to Indexed Color, follow these steps:

1. Choose "Export" from the File Menu, then select "GIF89a Export." You will get a dialog box for making transparency and interlacing choices.

2. Turn interlacing on or off using the checkbox.

3. Adobe's plug-in has an eyedropper for selecting a pixel color for transparency, which makes it a little easier to use than PhotoGIF. I've found that if I click on more than one pixel color, the effect is additive, meaning all the pixels of both colors will end up transparent. This feature was surprising at first, but may come in handy.

4. When you've selected your pixel color, click "OK."

5. Since this is an export function, Photoshop creates a new file, and adds a ".gif" suffix to the current filename (you can change it if you like). The new file will contain the transparency and interlacing information. The image you start with is unchanged.

DOWNLOAD IT!

Adobe's GIF89a plug-in to Photoshop for both Mac and WIndows is part of version 3.0.5, but if you have v.3.0.4, you can download the plug-in and upgrade directly off the Web at *http://www.adobe.com/Software.html*.

ten creating imagemaps

A
S WE MENTIONED IN CHAPTER 6, *What you need to know about Web graphics*, it is possible to create several links, or "hotspots," within a single graphic. These graphics are known as *imagemapped graphics* or *imagemaps*. The trick to putting lots of links in a graphic really has nothing to do with the graphic itself; it's just an ordinary GIF file. Rather, the graphic serves as a visual front-end to the mechanisms that match a particular pointer-click to a URL. There are a number of elements that make imagemaps work, and it gets into some pretty technical territory, so bear with me. It's important to know what's happening behind the scenes so that you can provide your share of the elements correctly.

■ HOW IMAGEMAPS WORK

Imagemapped graphics consist of the following elements working together:

- An inline graphic file.

- A map file, which resides on the server, containing all of the information necessary to match the position of a pointer click to a specific URL.

- A tag in the HTML file that tells the browser "this is an imagemapped graphic," along with directions on where to find the map file mentioned above.

- A CGI script (a sort of computer program) that runs on the server, or a built-in feature of either the server or client software that puts the pieces together and makes it work.

FIGURE 10-1 ▶

Cover graphic with "hotspots" highlighted

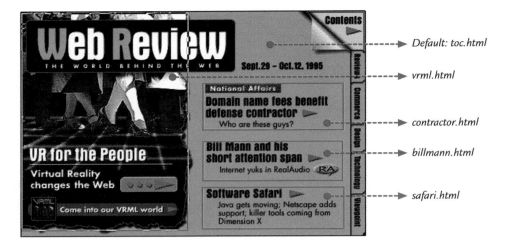

Default: toc.html

vrml.html

contractor.html

billmann.html

safari.html

▦ THE GRAPHIC FILE

Let's take a look at each of these parts in a little more detail. We'll begin with a graphic file—in this case, the "cover" graphic I designed for *Web Review*, an online magazine. The cover graphic is a large GIF file that lists some of the top stories within the magazine (Figure 10-1). I'd like the reader to be able to get to a story by clicking on its title. If someone happens to click somewhere outside one of my "hotspots," I'd like that person to link automatically to the Table of Contents page of the magazine.

The map file

Since there's nothing built into the graphic itself that tells the server which URL to link to when the user clicks, that information has to go *somewhere*. That's where the *map* file comes in. The map file, which stays on the server, matches pixel coordinates to the chosen URLs. Like HTML files, map files are simple text-only (ASCII) files. The map file starts by defining a default URL for any click that falls outside of one of the "hotspots." After that, each line in the map file contains the necessary information for one hotspot in the graphic, and it is made up of the following parts:

- *shape description:* the shape of a hotspot can be a rectangle, circle, or a polygon (denoted as "rect," "circle," or "poly" in the map file, respectively)

- *URL:* the absolute or relative URL* the area links to

- *list of pixel coordinates:* pairs of pixel positions (described by "x,y" or "over & down" coordinates), separated by spaces. The coordinates define the key points of the shape (the key points differ according to the shape they're describing).

The map file for my cover graphic, named "HOME.map," looks like this:

```
default toc.html
rect vrml.html 0,0 250,340
rect contractor.html 273,111 483,183
rect billmann.html 273,201 482,263
rect safari.html 272,273 484,338
```

The map file describes hotspot #1 (the VRML controversy) as a rectangle whose top-left pixel is located 0 pixels over and 0 pixels down, and whose bottom-right pixel is located 250 pixels over and 340 pixels down. If the cursor clicks within this area, the user will link to "vrml.html."

Since the map file is just a text file, you can edit it in any text editor to make changes to pathnames or pixel coordinates if necessary. And of course, if the dimensions or elements of the original graphic change, the coordinates in the map file need to be recalculated and changed.

Determining the sizes and shapes of the hotspots is generally a design decision, so chances are you will be responsible for creating the map files that accompany your graphics. You'll need to work with your server administrator (or some other contact person) to be sure that your map file gets incorporated into the server.

The map file contains some pretty nit-picky stuff to type out by hand (although I know many people do). Fortunately, you can find handy utilities out there that create map files automatically, and all you have to do is draw the shape and specify the URL.

I've always used a shareware utility for the Macintosh called *WebMap.* Windows users can use a similar program called *Mapedit.* At the end of this chapter, I'll do a step-by-step demo of how to use WebMap to create a map file. Like many other single-

*For more information on absolute vs. relative URLs, see pages 42–44 in Chapter 4, *Creating hypertext links*.

purpose Web utilities, the functionality of WebMap is being incorporated into larger graphics applications. Regardless of what you use to build your map file, the basic steps are likely to be the same.

The HTML instructions

There are a few tags you need to add to the HTML file to let the browser know that this is more than an ordinary graphic. Going back to our example, I needed to add the following tags to the HTML file for my cover page to make the imagemap work:

```
<A HREF="http://server.com/cgi-bin/imagemap/HOME.map">
<IMG SRC="cover.gif" ISMAP> </A>
```

Within the <IMG> tag, I've added the "ISMAP" attribute, which tells the browser that the graphic is intended to be an imagemap. Then I made the graphic a link to the map file, using the beginning and ending *anchor* <A> tags we've seen before and the map file's URL. Note here that the above example represents how I've tagged this imagemap to work on a UNIX server. The tagging format may differ from server to server, so it's best to get instructions from your server administrator for tagging your files correctly. That takes care of the HTML file. On to the server!

The server's role

Because this book is for designers, not programmers, your responsibility for making the imagemap work will probably end with the steps outlined above, but you should know that the process as a whole doesn't end there. The Web server needs to put all the pieces together, a job for the system administrator who maintains the server.

The server needs to have the map files installed correctly, either by copying them into a special directory or by running a program to incorporate them into the server.

Although you might be able to do this yourself, most likely you will need the server administrator to do it for you. Communicate with this person to let him or her know that you plan to use imagemaps in your Web site. It's extremely commonplace at this point, so it's unlikely you'll meet with any resistance, although running the script does require the server to work through an extra step or two.

Also, you should check with your administrator to find out in which server format

■ "CLIENT-SIDE" IMAGEMAPS

In the imagemap model I've used in this chapter, all the "magic" takes place on the server. For that reason, there is no way to test whether your map file is working correctly on your own machine (unless it doubles as a server). You need to wait until all the files are in place with the script before you can do any testing.

The latest development in imagemap technology is the "client-side" imagemap, a system for putting the necessary information right in the HTML file so that the work of matching coordinates to URLs occurs on the user's machine. As a result, the process is a lot faster, because the server is left out of the loop. This new way of handling things has a number of implications.

First, it means that you *would* be able to test your imagemap files without loading everything onto a server. It also enables users to view the URL that a hotspot links to by passing the cursor over it (usually, all you see is the coordinates). It would also permit working imagemaps to be stored on and used from a CD-ROM.

As of this writing, only Netscape and Spyglass Mosaic support this technology, but others are soon to follow.

to save your map file. The most common UNIX servers are the NCSA and the CERN server, which use different imagemap formats. It's best to check up front.

In addition, the administrator can be helpful in making sure that your files are organized properly and placed in the correct directories with the proper URLs linking them together.

■ KEEPING THE LOWEST COMMON DENOMINATOR IN MIND, AGAIN

Imagemaps are great tools for efficient and elegant Web page design, but you should use them responsibly. Think about what happens if, for some reason, the graphic doesn't show up. For example, say I place my spiffy imagemapped cover graphic on the first page of the *Web Review* site. From there, the reader has the Table of Contents and four linked stories to choose from.

But what happens if the user can't or has chosen not to display graphics in his or her browser? That person gets a useless "there's a graphic here" icon, or the word "image," and has no way of getting to the real meat of the site. All the linking options are hidden from them. They're stuck—definitely what I'd consider to be *non-functional*.

Now, you can provide some ALT text to describe what's happening in the graphic, but unfortunately, you can only link that text to one place. That means in our example above, three of the four links would still be unavailable.

The only alternative is to repeat those links in text somewhere on the page so all users have access to them. The use of imagemapped graphics requires a certain level of redundancy if you care about your entire audience.

On the *Web Review* cover page, I've typed out the story titles in the HTML text and linked them to the stories (Figure 10-2). That way, readers get to a story even if the graphic doesn't display. It's a bit clunky, and you'd probably never do something like this in any other medium. But hey, this is the Web.

If you're maintaining a separate "text-only" version of your site, you may decide that non-graphical browsers are taken care of well enough in that space, so you could keep your graphical version free of redundant text.

FIGURE 10-2 ▶

*Links within the imagemap are repeated in text
for users who can't view the graphics.*

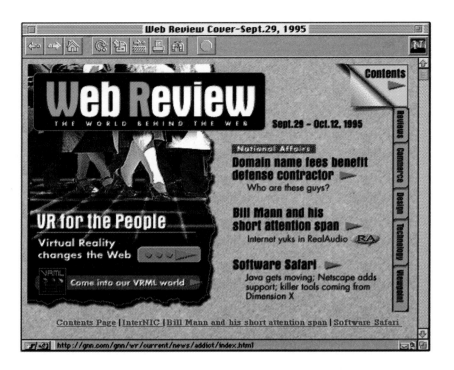

Another alternative, if you really don't want to devote space on your page for a list of redundant links, is to link the ALT text to the *most desirable* next page. I may decide that the Table of Contents page is the most important link out of the five, since all of the stories can be accessed from there.

So, users without the benefit of graphics may not get *all* the navigation options that the graphical version offers, but it's important that they can go *somewhere*.

Creating map files

 TOOLS: WebMap, version 2.0b

> **D O W N L O A D   I T !**
>
> You can get a copy of WebMap directly off the Web. Point your browser at *http://www.city.net/cnx/software/webmap.html.* Windows users can try Mapedit (*http://www.boutell.com/mapedit/*).

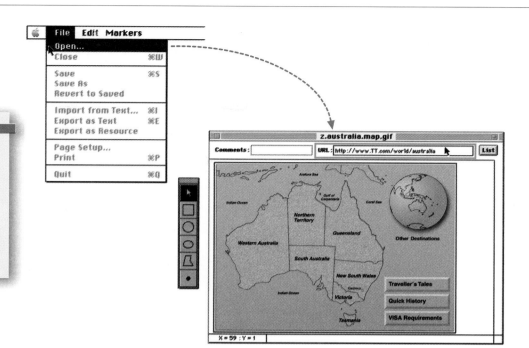

1. Open your GIF file in WebMap (versions prior to 2.0 can only open graphics in the PICT format). The graphic file is used like a template for laying out the hotspots. It isn't altered or saved in any way.

2. First, set the default link by typing the URL in the box at the top of the window and hitting "Return."

3. Choose the shape tool that best matches the shape of the hotspot you'd like to create. The tools work similarly to the shape tools in a simple drawing program such as Freehand or Illustrator.

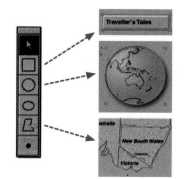

URL : http://www.TT.com/world/australia/tales

URL : http://www.TT.com/world

URL : http://www.TT.com/world/australia/ns.wales

4. Create one hotspot at a time by placing a square or circle, or by tracing an irregular shape with the polygon tool. Once you've created the shape, you can select it and move it around or make changes to its dimensions.

5. With the shape selected, type the URL for the link in the text-entry box at the top of the window.

6. Repeat steps 3 and 4 for each clickable area on the imagemap.

7. When you have created all of your hotspots, you need to save the information you've created as a text file. Do this by selecting "Export as Text" from the File menu. You need to name the text file with the ".map" suffix (unless your server administrator specifies otherwise). WebMap creates a text file that lists each shape, the pixel coordinates that define it, and the URL it links to.

A few notes:

Because WebMap doesn't actually change the graphic itself, there is no need to re-save it.

To view the map file, you need to open it in a text editing program.

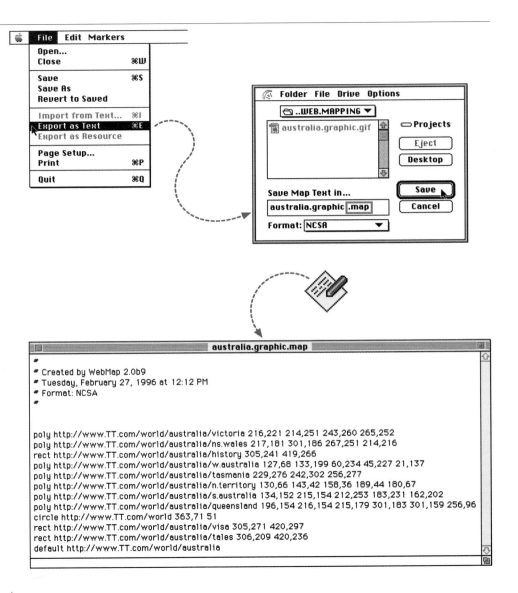

the rest of the page

eleven a designer's guide to html

N CHAPTER 1, *How the Web works*, I introduced you to the concept of HTML but promised not to bog you down with the details until later. Well, here's where I make good on that promise to get down to the nitty-gritty!

As you know, every element you see on a Web page is the result of an HTML tag. These tags are really the only tools we have as designers for making a page look a certain way. Unfortunately, HTML tags were never intended to be *design* tools in the first place, but rather just a way for scientists to share data with their colleagues around the world. As a designer, you may feel like you're fighting the medium every step of the way.

Although, you may not need to become a tagging expert, I still advocate that designers learn enough HTML to build basic Web pages and to know the limits of what can be done online. I'm fortunate enough to work with a production team that is responsible for building the final HTML files for the documents I design. When I create a graphics package for a particular story or site, I'll generally plug it into an HTML "sketch" to show the production person how I intend the graphics to be used. Most designers I've talked to intend to hire people to handle HTML markup for them, but they are still interested in learning what the language can and cannot do.

If you are hell-bent on becoming an expert, this chapter isn't going to get you there. There are plenty of fine and hefty books that treat the topic more comprehensively than I will here. I'd like to introduce you to some of the most commonly used HTML tags and what they do, paying special attention to the tags I use most often to affect how my Web page *looks*. I've divided the tags into the following groups, which are somewhat different than how they are perceived by the HTML development community, but I find it makes them easier to reference as design tools:

- Tags that set up the document (page 118)

- Tags that affect text (pages 119–125)

- The image tag and its attributes (pages 126–128)

- Tags that affect elements on the page (pages 129–132)

- A tag to aid in navigation (page 133)

- Tags that affect backgrounds (pages 134–136)

- Tags that affect text color (page 137)

■ LEARNING HTML

With new tools available, such as Adobe's PageMill, that potentially spare you from ever having to deal with HTML in constructing your Web pages, you may wonder why you'd need to learn HTML at all. Eventually, I don't think you will, but I also don't believe that we're at that point quite yet. You can't get very far right now as a Web page designer without a basic knowledge of HTML.

One reason why you need to know some HTML is that the WYSIWYG page-building tools are still in their infancy. As of this printing, PageMill only supports the limited HTML 2.0 standard, which means if you want to wrap text around a graphic, you're going to need to open the source HTML file in a text editor and add those tags manually. In addition, the general consensus in the field is that the HTML files that PageMill generates are not of professional quality.

Also, I think you will be glad to be able to look at an HTML source file and understand what you're looking at. Say you see a really cool Web page, and you want to know how the designer created a certain alignment trick. You can always "View Source" to see how it's done, but if the source looks like a bunch of gibberish to you, it won't do you much good. Sort of the way I feel when I look under the hood of my car for the source of that rattling noise.

The best way to learn HTML tags is not to read about them but to play around with them. Create a text document and see what you can make it do in HTML. If you don't like what you've got, move some tags around, save, then reload. Keep experimenting until you get a feel for what you can do, or perhaps more importantly, *can't* do, with the tags.

Chapter 3, *Assembling a Web page*, provided some step-by-step information on how to construct a typical HTML file. Consider the list of tag descriptions in the current chapter as a sort of ingredient list. Unless otherwise noted, all examples are displayed in the Netscape browser.

Tags that set up the document

\<HTML>\</HTML>

The \<HTML> tags tell the browser that the contents they contain should be rendered as an HTML file.

\<HEAD>\</HEAD>

The header portion is used to contain information about the document that is used by the browser but generally not displayed to the user in the Web page itself. In this example, I am using the header to contain the title of my document, explained below.

\<TITLE>\</TITLE>

The text between these tags is the title of the document. Browsers have different ways of displaying titles, but most often, they'll appear in a bar at the top of the browser window. The title may also be used in the document's "info" window (if your browser supports one), and in the bookmarks (or hotspots) list that you create using your browser (Figure 11-1).

\<BODY>\</BODY>

The material between these tags is displayed in the browser window.

he first set of tags you need to know are used to establish the document as an HTML file and to organize its contents. I think of these as "structural" tags, and they are generally the first tags I add to a document. Many HTML editors have a function that adds them all in one fell swoop. These tags were outlined previously in Chapter 3, but I'll review them here as the first step in setting up an HTML document to play with throughout this chapter.

Remember that browsers don't recognize returns and spaces, so you may notice that I use them liberally in the example HTML documents to keep the elements clear. Many people also use spaces to indent different levels of information, an old programmers' trick for making the file easier to read.

▼ FIGURE 11-1: *"Structural" tags*

```
<HTML>

<HEAD>
<TITLE>United States Constitution</TITLE>
</HEAD>

<BODY>
Preamble...
</BODY>

</HTML>
```

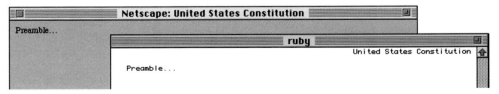

Tags that affect text

■ BREAKING LINES

<P>

Paragraph break: this tag is like adding a "return." It breaks the line and adds a little space between paragraphs (Figure 11-2). The browser will not recognize more than one consecutive <P> tag, so you can't use a string of them to add extra space between elements, the way you can in a word processing program (Figure 11-3).

In the HTML specification, the paragraph tag has a corresponding "end paragraph" tag, </P>, but in practice it is rarely used.

Break: This tag breaks the line but doesn't add any extra space (Figure 11-4).

▼ FIGURE 11-2: *Paragraph tag*

```
Preamble
<P>
We, the people of the United States, in order to form a more perfect
Union...
```

Preamble

We, the people of the United States, in order to form a more perfect Union...

▼ FIGURE 11-3: *Multiple paragraph tags*

```
Preamble
<P>
<P>
<P>
We, the people of the United States, in order to form a more perfect
Union...
```

Preamble

We, the people of the United States, in order to form a more perfect Union...

▼ FIGURE 11-4: *Break tag*

```
Preamble
<BR>
We, the people of the United States, in order to form a more perfect
Union...
```

Preamble
We, the people of the United States, in order to form a more perfect Union...

\<H#>\</H#>

Headings are generally displayed in bold text with an automatic line break at the end and space added above and below. The "**#**" can equal one through six (Figure 11-5):

\<H1>\</H1>

First-level heading: text placed between these tags is generally set in the large, bold type.

\<H2>\</H2>

Second-level heading: text placed between these tags is generally displayed in bold type that is slightly smaller than the first-level headings.

Note: Third, fourth, fifth, and sixth level headings are displayed in consecutively smaller bold type. By the time browsers get down to the \<H5> level, they tend to display the text even smaller than regular text, and it can be difficult to read. As a general rule, \<H3> is as low as you'd want to go, but many people use \<H5> for "small print," such as photo credits or copyright notices.

Be sure to remember to close your heading tags, or your whole document will be displayed in large, bold type.

▼ FIGURE 11-5: *Heading tags*

```
<H1>United States Constitution</H1>

<H2>Preamble</H2>
We, the people of the United States, in order to form a more perfect
Union...

<H2>Article I</H2>

<H3>Section 1.</H3>
Legislative powers; in whom vested. All legislative powers herein
granted shall be vested in a Congress of the United States, which shall
consist of a Senate and House of Representatives.

<H5>written in 1789</H5>
```

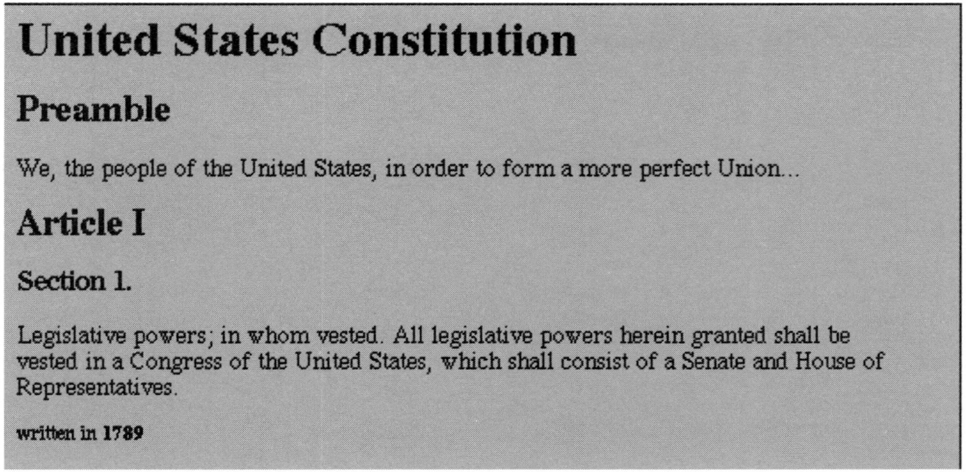

United States Constitution

Preamble

We, the people of the United States, in order to form a more perfect Union...

Article I

Section 1.

Legislative powers; in whom vested. All legislative powers herein granted shall be vested in a Congress of the United States, which shall consist of a Senate and House of Representatives.

written in 1789

◼ STYLED TEXT

<I></I>

Italic text: (Figure 11-6) this tag is an example of a "physical" tag, which gives specific display instructions, in this case, specifying italic text. Use italic text sparingly, as most browsers just oblique the text font to achieve an "italic." The result is often nearly unreadable, especially in large quantities of text.

<B></B>

Bold text: this tag specifies bold text (Figure 11-6)

<EM></EM>

Emphasized text: (Figure 11-7) this tag is an example of a "logical" HTML tag. Most browsers display emphasized text in italics. .

<STRONG></STRONG>

Strong text: (Figure 11-7) most browsers will render type between this logical tag in bold. Again, if you want to be sure, use the physical <B> tag.

▼ FIGURE 11-6: *Bold and italic*

<B>We, the people of the United States</B>, in order to form a more perfect Union, establish justice, insure domestic tranquility, provide for the common defense, promote the general welfare, and secure the blessings of liberty to ourselves and our posterity, do ordain and establish this <I>Constitution for the United States of America</I>.

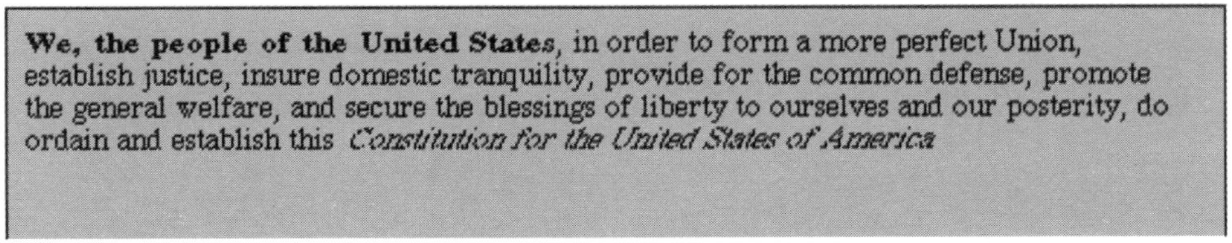

We, the people of the United States, in order to form a more perfect Union, establish justice, insure domestic tranquility, provide for the common defense, promote the general welfare, and secure the blessings of liberty to ourselves and our posterity, do ordain and establish this *Constitution for the United States of America*

▼ FIGURE 11-7: *Strong and emphasized*

<STRONG>We, the people of the United States</STRONG>, in order to form a more perfect Union, establish justice, insure domestic tranquility, provide for the common defense, promote the general welfare, and secure the blessings of liberty to ourselves and our posterity, do ordain and establish this <EM>Constitution for the United States of America</EM>.

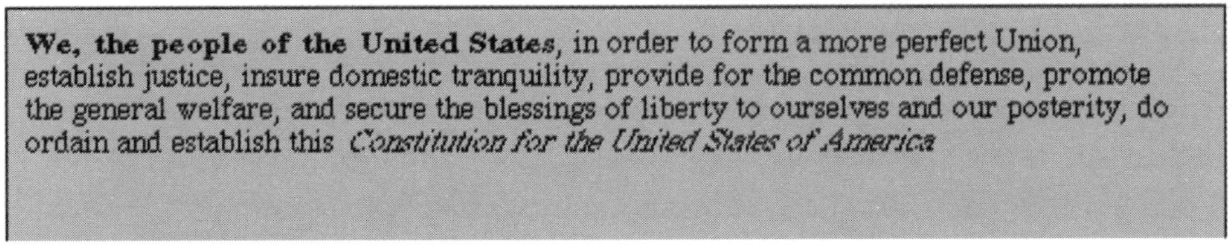

We, the people of the United States, in order to form a more perfect Union, establish justice, insure domestic tranquility, provide for the common defense, promote the general welfare, and secure the blessings of liberty to ourselves and our posterity, do ordain and establish this *Constitution for the United States of America*

■ LISTS

`<LI>`

List item: each item in a list needs to be preceded by an `<LI>` tag. You can experiment with adding `<P>`s to get the spacing effect you like above and below items. (Figure 11-8 uses paragraph breaks.) You can also insert `<P>` tags to create multiple paragraphs within a single list item. `<LI>` tags must be used in conjunction with either of the list designations explained below.

`<UL></UL>` with `<LI>`

"Unordered" or "Unnumbered" list: Unordered lists are almost always set as bulleted lists (Figure 11-8). The bullets are added automatically by the browser, and items in the list are usually set on an indent. The `<UL>` tag goes at the beginning of the list, and `</UL>` goes at the very end to turn the list function "off." The `<LI>` tag precedes each item on the list.

`<OL></OL>` with `<LI>`

Ordered list: this list is the same as a numbered list (Figure 11-9). Browsers automatically will put a number before each list item and set each item on an indent. Ordered lists also require the `<LI>` tag before each item in the list.

▼ FIGURE 11-8: *Unordered list*

Section 2. House of Representatives, how and by whom chosen Qualifications of a Representative...**`<P>`**
`<UL>`
`<LI>`The House of Representatives shall be composed of members chosen every second year by the people of the several States...**`<P>`**
`<LI>`No person shall be a Representative...**`<P>`**
`<LI>`Representatives [and direct taxes]...
`</UL>`

Section 2. House of Representatives, how and by whom chosen Qualifications of a Representative...

- The House of Representatives shall be composed of members chosen every second year by the people of the several States...

- No person shall be a Representative...

▼ FIGURE 11-9: *Ordered list*

Section 2. House of Representatives, how and by whom chosen Qualifications of a Representative...**`<P>`**
`<OL>`
`<LI>`The House of Representatives shall be composed of members chosen every second year by the people of the several States...
`<LI>`No person shall be a Representative...
`<LI>`Representatives [and direct taxes]...
`</OL>`

Section 2. House of Representatives, how and by whom chosen Qualifications of a Representative...

1. The House of Representatives shall be composed of members chosen every second year by the people of the several States...
2. No person shall be a Representative...
3. Representatives [and direct taxes]...

\<DL>\</DL>

Dictionary list: these tags are used for displaying lists of words with blocks of descriptive text (Figure 11-10). The \<DL>\</DL> tags indicate the beginning and end of the list.

\<DT>

Dictionary term: this tag marks the word to be defined. Browsers usually position this word against the left margin; some browsers will render it in bold type. If you want it to be bold for sure, add \<B> tags around the term as shown in Figure 11-10.

\<DD>

Dictionary definition: browsers generally start the definition on a new line, aligned on an indent. Since there isn't any other way to create indents in HTML 2.0, the dictionary list (especially in several nested levels) has become the classic fudge for creating indented text. It's poor form, but it works.

▼ FIGURE 11-10: *Dictionary lists*

```
<DL>
<DT><B>Section 1.</B>
<DD>Legislative powers; in whom vested. All legislative powers herein
granted shall be vested in a Congress of the United States, which shall
consist of a Senate and House of Representatives.<P>
<DT><B>Section 2.</B>
<DD>House of Representatives, how and by whom chosen. Qualifica-
tions of a Representative. Representatives and direct taxes, how appor-
tioned. Enumeration. Vacancies to be filled. Power of choosing officers,
and of impeachment. <P>
<DT><B>Section 3.</B>
<DD>Senators, how and by whom chosen. How classified. State Execu-
tive, when to make temporary appointments, in case, etc. Qualifications
of a Senator. President of the Senate, his right to vote. President pro
tem., and other officers of the Senate, how chosen. Power to try
impeachments. When President is tried, Chief Justice to preside.
</DL>
```

Section 1.
   Legislative powers; in whom vested. All legislative powers herein granted shall be vested in a Congress of the United States, which shall consist of a Senate and House of Representatives.

Section 2.
   House of Representatives, how and by whom chosen. Qualifications of a Representative. Representatives and direct taxes, how apportioned. Enumeration. Vacancies to be filled. Power of choosing officers, and of impeachment.

Section 3.
   Senators, how and by whom chosen. How classified. State Executive, when to make temporary appointments, in case, etc. Qualifications of a Senator. President of the Senate, his right to vote. President pro tem., and other officers of the Senate, how chosen. Power to try impeachments. When President is tried, Chief Justice to preside.

■ ADDITIONAL TEXT FORMATTING TAGS:

`<BLOCKQUOTE></BLOCKQUOTE>`

Quotations: blockquotes are generally displayed with an indent on the left and right margins with a little extra space added above and below (Figure 11-11). For this reason, they are frequently used as a fudge to create narrow columns of text. Beware that some browsers render blockquoted material all in italics, making it very difficult to read.

`<TT></TT>`

Typewriter text: text between these tags will be displayed in the fixed-width (constant-width) font that is specified by the browser. Most browsers use Courier as the default fixed-width font (Figure 11-12).

`<PRE></PRE>`

Preformatted text: these tags will also display text in the fixed-width font, but with an important difference. In preformatted text, carriage returns, multiple character spaces, and tabs are recognized by the browser (remember that browsers usually ignore these things). With this tag, you can control spacing and line length exactly (as long as you don't mind everything set in Courier or an equivalent) (Figure 11-12).

▼ FIGURE 11-11: *Blockquote*

```
AMENDMENT V <P>
<BLOCKQUOTE>No person shall be held to answer for a capital, or oth-
erwise infamous crime, unless on a presentment or indictment of a
Grand Jury, except in cases arising in the land or naval forces, or in the
militia, when in actual service in time of war or public
danger;...</BLOCKQUOTE>
```

AMENDMENT V

No person shall be held to answer for a capital, or otherwise infamous crime, unless on a presentment or indictment of a Grand Jury, except in cases arising in the land or naval forces, or in the militia, when in actual service in time of war or public danger;...

▼ FIGURE 11-12: *Typewriter text vs. preformatted text*

```
<TT>AMENDMENT VIII<BR>
Excessive bail shall not be required,
nor excessive fines imposed, nor cruel
and unusual punishments inflicted.</TT>
<P>
<PRE>AMENDMENT IX
The enumeration in the Constitution, of certain
rights, shall not be construed to deny or disparage
others retained by the people.</PRE>
```

AMENDMENT VIII
Excessive bail shall not be required, nor excessive fines imposed, nor cruel and unusual punishments inflicted.

AMENDMENT IX
    The enumeration in the Constitution, of certain
    rights, shall not be construed to deny or disparage
    others retained by the people.

<FONT SIZE=x></FONT>*

Font size: this extension tag changes the relative size of the font. The value can be set from 1 to 7, with 3 being the default size. Alternatively, you can specify a value that is "+" or "–" a value relative to the basefont size (Figure 11-13). (Author's note: this whole 1 to 7 number system is baffling to me. I'm not quite sure how it translates to the more familiar language of describing font size in points. If you are interested in using this tag, it's best to experiment with it until the font looks the way you want it and don't worry so much about the actual point size.) I've seen many online publications raise the font value "+1" in the attempt to make large amounts of text easier to read on the screen. Beware that enlarged type often looks clunky and less readable, especially on Macs for some reason.

<BASEFONT SIZE=x>*

Basefont size: this extension establishes the basefont size on which all text in the document is based. The default basefont size is 3, and it can be reduced by setting a value of 1 or 2, or enlarged by specifying a value of 4 to 7. Headings will be affected as well, since they are calculated proportionally from the basefont (Figure 11-14).

*Not part of the HTML 2.0 spec; therefore, this tag may not be supported by all browsers.

▼ FIGURE 11-13: *Font size tag*

```
<H2>Preamble</H2>

<FONT SIZE=+2>We, the people of the United States,</FONT> in order
to form a more perfect Union, establish justice, insure domestic tran-
quility, provide for the common defense, promote the general welfare,
and secure the blessings of liberty to ourselves and our posterity, do
ordain and establish this Constitution for the United States of America.
```

Preamble

We, the people of the United States, in order to form a more perfect Union, establish justice, insure domestic tranquility, provide for the common defense, promote the general welfare, and secure the blessings of liberty to ourselves and our posterity, do ordain and establish this Constitution for the United States of America.

▼ FIGURE 11-14: *Basefont tag (with font tag)*

```
<BASEFONT SIZE=4>
<H2>Preamble</H2>
<FONT SIZE=+2>We, the people of the United States,</FONT> in order
to form a more perfect Union, establish justice, insure domestic tran-
quility, provide for the common defense, promote the general welfare,
and secure the blessings of liberty to ourselves and our posterity, do
ordain and establish this Constitution for the United States of America.
```

Preamble

We, the people of the United States, in order to form a more perfect Union, establish justice, insure domestic tranquility, provide for the common defense, promote the general welfare, and secure the blessings of liberty to ourselves and our posterity, do ordain and establish this Constitution for the United States of America.

The image tag and its attributes

<IMG...>

Image tag: this is the basic tag that tells the browser "place a graphic here." The rest of the tags in this section are attributes that can be placed within the <IMG> tag to give the browser more complete instructions on handling the image. In standard HTML 2.0, graphics are placed against the left margin with a maximum of one line of type next to them (Figure 11-15). If I had wanted the graphic to appear on a line by itself, I would need to insert a paragraph tag to break the line.

SRC="graphic name (or URL that points to graphic)"

Source: this attribute specifies the name of the graphic file to place on the page. The pathname or complete URL that points to it may also be included.

ALT="text here"

Alternative text: text placed in this attribute will appear on the page when the graphic is not displayed. It is a good way to make sure people viewing your page on a text-only browser (or on a browser with the graphics turned off) will get the basic message of the page.

▼ FIGURE 11-15: *Image tag with alternative text*

```
<H2>Preamble</H2>
<P>
<IMG SRC="flag.gif" ALT="[United States Flag]">
We, the people of the United States, in order to form a more perfect
Union, establish justice, insure domestic tranquility, provide for the
common defense, promote the general welfare, and secure the bless-
ings of liberty to ourselves and our posterity, do ordain and establish
this Constitution for the United States of America.
```

On a graphical browser

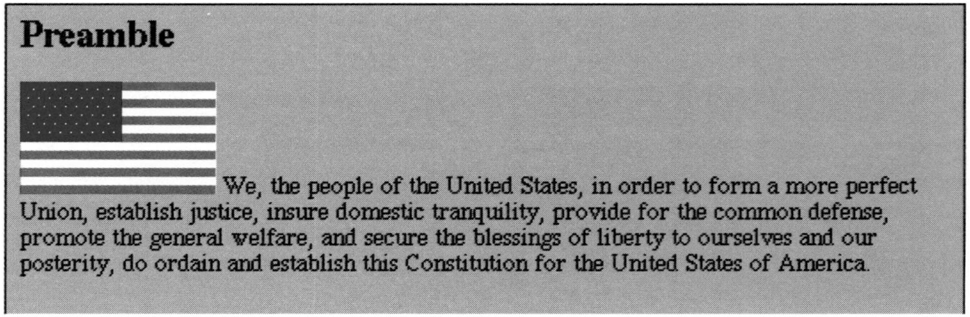

On a non-graphical browser

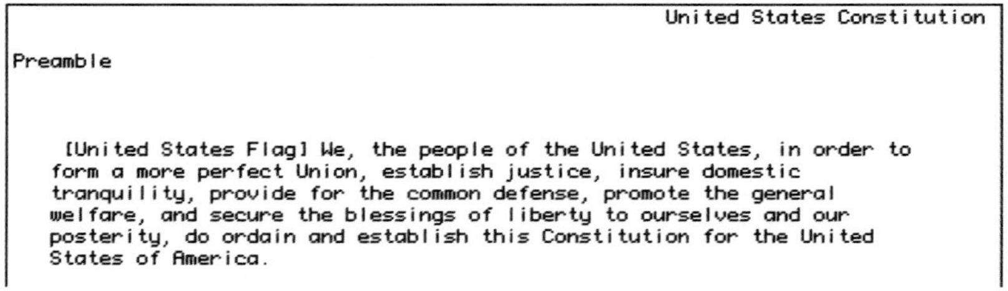

ALIGN=left or **right***

This attribute positions a graphic against the left or right margin of the page. It also allows text to wrap around the image (Figure 11-16).

HSPACE=x*

Horizontal space: this attribute will insert a specified number of pixels to the left and right of the image. It prevents text from bumping right up against a graphic which has been aligned left or right (Figure 11-17).

VSPACE=x*

Vertical space: this attribute is similar to horizontal space, except it controls space above and below the graphic.

WIDTH=x and **HEIGHT=x***

Width and height: this information specifies the graphic's size, measured in pixels. The browser can use this information to reserve an area of space for the graphic to fill while it continues downloading the file and formatting the page. It doesn't necessarily affect the way the page looks, but rather is a way to make the final page download up to 50% faster. Note that if you specify a width or height that is different from your graphic's measurements, some browsers such as Netscape will resize your graphic to the specified size. Although this is a tempting feature to use, it means that the quality of your page is at the mercy of the browser's rendering capabilities.

*Not part of the HTML 2.0 spec; therefore, this tag may not be supported by all browsers.

▼ FIGURE 11-16: *Graphic alignment*

```
<H2>Preamble</H2>
<P>
<IMG SRC="flag.gif" ALIGN=left>
We, the people of the United States, in order to form a more perfect
Union, establish justice, insure domestic tranquility, provide for the
common defense, promote the general welfare, and secure the bless-
ings of liberty to ourselves and our posterity, do ordain and establish
this Constitution for the United States of America.
```

▼ FIGURE 11-17: *Graphic alignment with horizontal space*

```
<H2>Preamble</H2>
<P>
<IMG SRC="flag.gif" ALIGN=left HSPACE=10>
We, the people of the United States,...
```

BORDER=x*

Border: the border attribute affects the blue line that appears by default around a linked graphic. The value entered after the border attribute represents how many pixels wide the blue border will be. For instance, BORDER=3 will make the blue border 3 pixels wide. Setting a zero as the value will turn the border off completely. This is a nifty tool for linked graphics with transparent edges. Having a blue rectangle around a transparent image defeats the purpose and also looks a little silly (Figure 11-18).

ISMAP

Imagemap: this tag tells the browser that the graphic is an imagemap. For more information on imagemaps, see Chapter 10, *Creating imagemaps.*

▼ FIGURE 11-18: *Border setting*

```
<H2>Preamble</H2>
<P>
<A HREF="document.html"><IMG SRC="flag.gif" BORDER=3></A>
<P>
We, the people of the United States, in order to form a more perfect
Union, establish justice,...
```

```
...<A HREF="document.html"><IMG SRC="flag2.gif" BORDER=0></A>...
```

*Not part of the HTML 2.0 spec; therefore, these tags may not be supported by all browsers.

Tags that affect elements on the page

■ TAGS FOR POSITIONING

<BR CLEAR=ALL>*

Break and clear all: this tag is useful when you have graphics aligned against the left or right margin. The "clear-all" attribute not only breaks the line, but it holds empty space next to the graphic until it gets to the bottom edge. The next text element will be displayed below the graphic (Figure 11-19).

If you had large pictures with short captions, you might want to use the "break and clear all" attribute to make sure the following text doesn't stack up next to the first image. Compare Figure 11-19 to Figure 11-20.

▼ FIGURE 11-19: *Break and clear all*

```
<IMG SRC=smallflag.gif ALIGN=left HPACE=6>
<B>Section 1.</B><BR>
Legislative powers...
<BR CLEAR=ALL>

<B>Section 2.</B>
House of Representatives, how and by whom chosen...
```

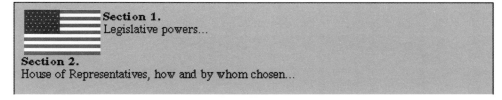

▼ FIGURE 11-20: *Same page without "Break and clear all" tag*

```
<IMG SRC=smallflag.gif ALIGN=left HPACE=6>
<B>Section 1.</B><BR>
Legislative powers...

<B>Section 2.</B>
House of Representatives, how and by whom chosen...
```

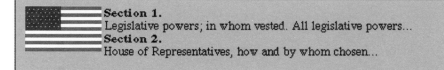

*Not part of the HTML 2.0 spec; therefore, this tag may not be supported by all browsers.

`<NOBR></NOBR>`*

No break: text and graphics that appear within this tag will always appear on one line, which will not be broken by the automatic wrapping function of the browser window (Figure 11-21). If the string of elements within this tag is very long, it will continue off the browser page and users will have to scroll to the right to see it.

I often use the no-break tag to hold together a string of graphics that I'd like to be viewed as one piece. For example, recall my fake home page in Chapter 1, which fared so poorly when a user changed the width of the browser window. (See Figure 2-2 on page 15.) If I add <NOBR> tags around the three graphics that make up the masthead, they will always appear on the same line, regardless of how narrow the user has set the browser. The part that doesn't fit just won't be visible (Figure 11-22).

▼ FIGURE 11-21: *The no-break tag*

```
<H1>Preamble</H1>
<NOBR>We, the people of the United States, in order to form a more
perfect Union, establish justice, insure domestic tranquility, provide for
the common defense, promote the general welfare, and secure the
blessings of liberty to ourselves and our posterity, do ordain and estab-
lish this Constitution for the United States of America.</NOBR>
```

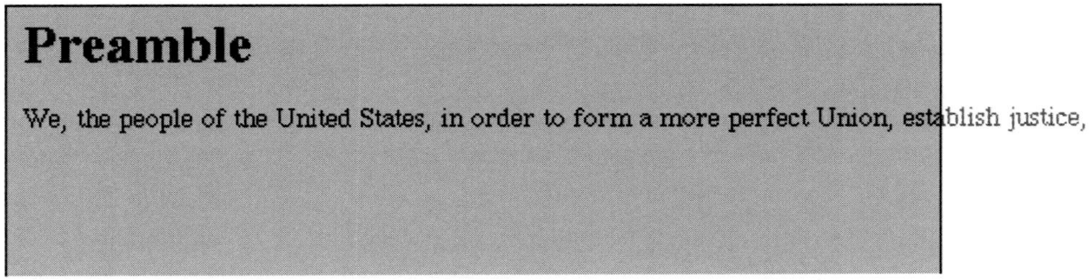

Preamble

We, the people of the United States, in order to form a more perfect Union, establish justice,

▼ FIGURE 11-22: *Another example of the no-break tag*

```
<NOBR><IMG SRC="star.gif"><IMG SRC="jenbanner.gif"><IMG
SRC="star.gif"></NOBR>
<CENTER><H1>Welcome to my Web Page</H1></CENTER>
```

*Not part of the HTML 2.0 spec; therefore, this tag may not be supported by all browsers.

<CENTER></CENTER>*

Center tag: everything that falls within these tags will be centered in the browser window. You can use it to center specific headlines, graphics, lines of text, or entire pages (Figure 11-23). Basically, it will start centering elements until the tag is turned off, so you can put as many or as few elements between them as you please.

The center tag is another instance where the convention doesn't follow the true HTML 3.0 spec. In the spec, the correct tag for centering is **<P ALIGN="CENTER">**, although it is rarely used. Netscape first introduced the **<CENTER>** tag as part of their extensions to HTML 2.0, and their less-than-kosher format has just caught on.

*Not part of the HTML 2.0 spec; therefore, this tag may not be supported by all browsers.

▼ FIGURE 11-23: *Centering*

```
<CENTER><B>Section 1.</B></CENTER>
<IMG SRC=smallflag.gif><P>
Legislative powers; in whom vested. All legislative powers herein
granted shall be vested in a Congress of the United States, which shall
consist of a Senate and House of Representatives.
<P>

<CENTER>
<B>Section 2.</B>
<IMG SRC=smallflag.gif><P>
House of Representatives, how and by whom chosen. Qualifications of a
Representative. Representatives and direct taxes, how apportioned.
Enumeration. Vacancies to be filled. Power of choosing officers, and of
impeachment.
</CENTER>
```

Section 1.

Legislative powers; in whom vested. All legislative powers herein granted shall be vested in a Congress of the United States, which shall consist of a Senate and House of Representatives.

Section 2.

House of Representatives, how and by whom chosen. Qualifications of a Representative. Representatives and direct taxes, how apportioned. Enumeration. Vacancies to be filled. Power of choosing officers, and of impeachment.

▪ RULES

<HR>

Horizontal rule: this tag will insert a horizontal line on the page. You can add a paragraph tag <P> above and/or below the horizontal rule to give it a little more space (Fig. 11-24). Browsers have different ways of rendering this rule, so it could be a black line of a single pixel-width or a shaded gray line with a 3-D shadow effect.

Netscape created the following additional attributes that go within the rule tag and give the designer more control (Figure 11-25).

SIZE=x*

This attribute specifies rule thickness in pixels.

WIDTH=x or %*

This attribute determines how many pixels wide (or a percentage of the page width) the rule should be. By default, the rule is the full width of the browser window.

ALIGN=left/right/center*

If the rule is shorter than the window width, this tag gives control over placement.

NOSHADE*

In Netscape, rules are shaded. This attribute guarantees the rule will be displayed as a solid bar.

*Not part of the HTML 2.0 spec; therefore, these tags may not be supported by all browsers.

▼ FIGURE 11-24: *Horizontal rules*

```
<B>ARTICLE I</B>
<P><HR>
Section 1. Legislative powers; in whom vested. All legislative powers
herein granted shall be vested in a Congress of the United States, which
shall consist of a Senate and House of Representatives.
<HR>
Section 2. House of Representatives, how and by whom chosen. Qualifi-
cations of a Representative. Representatives and direct taxes, how
apportioned. Enumeration. Vacancies to be filled. Power of choosing
officers, and of impeachment.
<HR>
```

ARTICLE I

Section 1. Legislative powers; in whom vested. All legislative powers herein granted shall be vested in a Congress of the United States, which shall consist of a Senate and House of Representatives.

Section 2. House of Representatives, how and by whom chosen. Qualifications of a Representative. Representatives and direct taxes, how apportioned. Enumeration. Vacancies to be filled. Power of choosing officers, and of impeachment.

▼ FIGURE 11-25: *Horizonal rule with Netscape attributes*

```
Section 1. Legislative powers; in whom vested...
<HR SIZE=2 WIDTH=75% ALIGN=center>
Section 2. House of Representatives, how and by whom chosen...
```

Section 1. Legislative powers; in whom vested...

Section 2. House of Representatives, how and by whom chosen...

A tag to aid in navigation

■ NAMED ANCHORS

You can create links to specific points or sections within a document (Figure 11-26). For instance, if you have a long scrolling document, you can provide a list of links at the top that drop you down to the appropriate section when you click on that section's title.

<A NAME="[text]"></A>

This "named anchor" tag gives the material it contains a name that can be referenced elsewhere. It's like putting a marker in the file so you can get back to it easily.

To link to this marker, you use a regular anchor tag (see Chapter 4 for more on anchor tags). The name from the above tag needs to be referenced in this way:

<A HREF="#[text]">link</A>

You can also link to the marker from another document, but you have to include the filename and the anchor name in the tag:

<A HREF="story.html#[text]"> link</A>

▼ FIGURE 11-26: *Named anchors*

```
<H1>United States Constitution</H1>

<A HREF="#pre">Preamble<A>
<A HREF="#art1>Article I</A>
<A HREF="#art2">Article II</A>
<A HREF-"#art3">Article III</A>

...


<A NAME="art2">Article II</A>
<P>
Section 1. President: his term of office. Electors of President; number
and how appointed. Electors to vote on same day. Qualification of Presi-
dent. On whom his duties devolve in case of his removal, death, etc.
President's compensation. His oath of office.
```

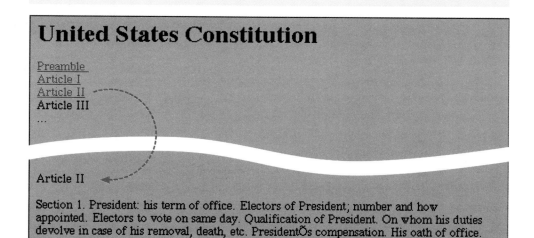

United States Constitution

Preamble
Article I
Article II
Article III
...

Article II

Section 1. President: his term of office. Electors of President; number and how appointed. Electors to vote on same day. Qualification of President. On whom his duties devolve in case of his removal, death, etc. PresidentÕs compensation. His oath of office.

Tags that affect backgrounds

■ TILED BACKGROUNDS

Tiled backgrounds are created by adding attributes within the <BODY> tag, as shown below.

<BODY BACKGROUND= "GIF"></BODY>*

Background tile tag: this tag will take the GIF file specified and use it as a repeating tiled background pattern. Use this effect with caution, as the wrong graphic can easily result in pages that are unreadable (as demonstrated in Figure 11-27). In addition, a very large graphic used as a tile will cause the page to load slowly.

▼ FIGURE 11-27: *Tiled backgrounds*

```
<HTML>
<BODY BACKGROUND="flag.gif">
<H1>Preamble</H1>
We, the people of the United States, in order to form a more perfect
Union, establish justice, insure domestic tranquility, provide for the
common defense, promote the general welfare, and secure the bless-
ings of liberty to ourselves and our posterity, do ordain and establish
this Constitution for the United States of America.
</BODY>
</HTML>
```

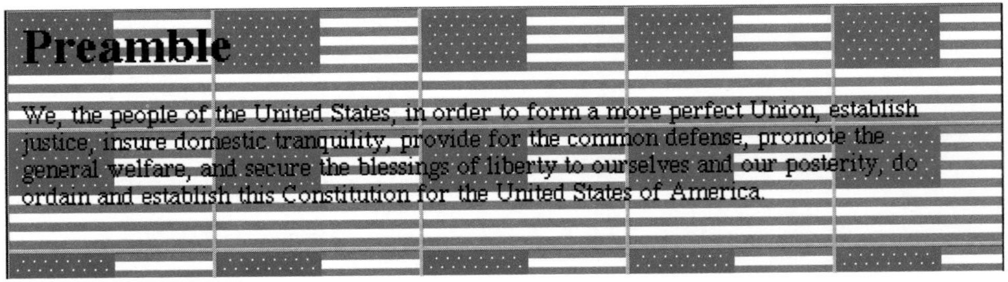

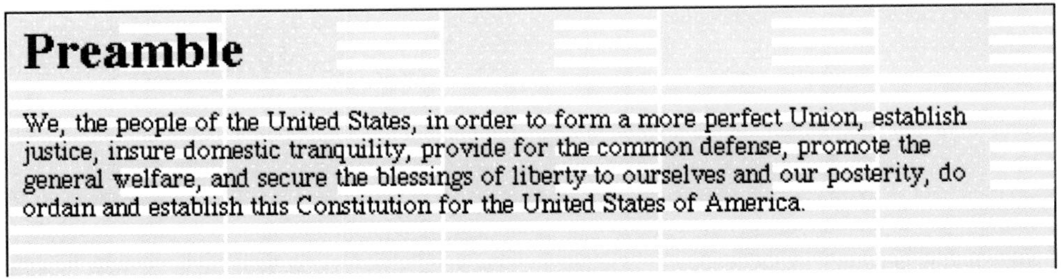

Preamble

We, the people of the United States, in order to form a more perfect Union, establish justice, insure domestic tranquility, provide for the common defense, promote the general welfare, and secure the blessings of liberty to ourselves and our posterity, do ordain and establish this Constitution for the United States of America.

Preamble

We, the people of the United States, in order to form a more perfect Union, establish justice, insure domestic tranquility, provide for the common defense, promote the general welfare, and secure the blessings of liberty to ourselves and our posterity, do ordain and establish this Constitution for the United States of America.

*Not part of the HTML 2.0 spec; therefore, this tag may not be supported by all browsers.

■ SOLID BACKGROUND COLORS

You can use the <BODY> tag of the HTML file to specify an RGB value to be used as the background color of the browser window, as shown below.

<BODY BGCOLOR="#RRGGBB"> </BODY>*

This attribute allows you to select a color to be used as a background color for the page. "RRGGBB" represents a "hexadecimal red-green-blue triplet used to specify a color." Let me explain this curious phrase more clearly.

1. Choose a color.

You need to describe the color by its RGB (red-green-blue) values. The red, green, and blue intensities are represented by numbers between 0 and 255. I use the "Color Picker" in Photoshop to choose a color and get its RGB values. For this example, I've chosen a shade of light blue with the following values (Figure 11-28): R=185; G=225; B=247.

2. Translate to hexadecimal value.

Second, to use this information in the tag, these decimal values need to be translated to their "hexadecimal" equivalents. The hexadecimal system is base sixteen instead of base ten (base ten is the

*Not part of HTML 2.0 spec; therefore, these tags may not be supported by all browsers.

▼ FIGURE 11-28: *Selecting a color by RGB values in Photoshop*

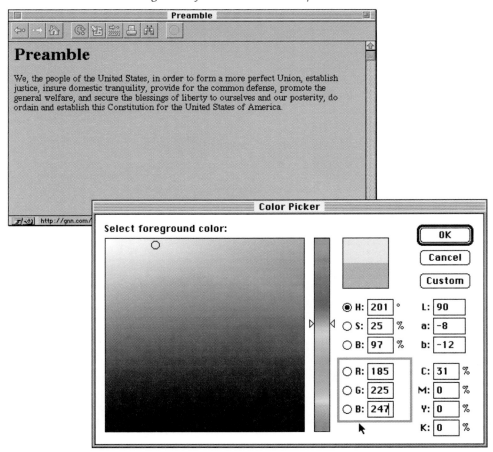

decimal system that we're used to). It uses the characters A through F to represent the decimal 10 through 15 equivalents. The hexadecimal system is widely used in computing to reduce the space it takes to store certain information (notice that the number of characters in our RGB values will be reduced from three to two).

You can calculate hex values by dividing your number by 16 to get the first number, and then use the remainder for the second number. So, 203=CB because 203=(16x12) + 11. That's {12, 11} in base 16, or CB in hexadecimal. Whew!

Or, you can do what I do and find a calculator that does the translation for you. I found one on the Net, which comes in handy. Also, if you are using BoxTop's PhotoGIF plug-in to Photoshop, the color dialog box handily displays the hexadecimal values for each pixel color in the image (Figure 11-29).

In hexadecimal, the RGB values for my off-white shade are: R=B9, G=E1, B=F7.

The resulting HTML tag to set my page to the chosen color is shown in Figure 11-30.

▼ FIGURE 11-29: *Translating RGB values to hexadecimal equivalents*

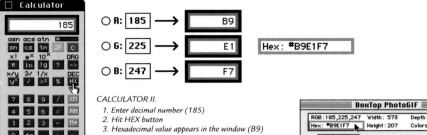

CALCULATOR II.
1. Enter decimal number (185)
2. Hit HEX button
3. Hexadecimal value appears in the window (B9)

Hexadecimal Fun Facts:

☐ White = FFFFFF

■ Black = 000000

▼ FIGURE 11-30:
Document with background color specified

```
<HTML>
<BODY BGCOLOR="#B9E1F7">
<H1>Preamble</H1>
We, the people of the United States, in order to form a more perfect
Union, establish justice, insure domestic tranquility, provide for the
common defense, promote the general welfare, and secure the bless-
ings of liberty to ourselves and our posterity, do ordain and establish
this Constitution for the United States of America.
</BODY>
</HTML>
```

Preamble

We, the people of the United States, in order to form a more perfect Union, establish justice, insure domestic tranquility, provide for the common defense, promote the general welfare, and secure the blessings of liberty to ourselves and our posterity, do ordain and establish this Constitution for the United States of America.

Tags that affect text color

■ SPECIFYING TEXT COLORS

You can use hexadecimal RGB values to specify text colors for a whole document within the <BODY> tag, too (Figure 11-31). The attributes are as follows:

TEXT="#RRGGBB"*

This attribute changes the color of all the normal text and headlines on the page. Text is black by default.

LINK="#RRGGBB"*

This attribute changes the color of link text. Linked text is blue by default. This blue has become a firmly established convention on the Web, and you should note that changing it may cause some confusion in using your page.

VLINK="#RRGGBB"*

This attribute changes the color of visited link (one you've already clicked on). Visited links are purple by default.

To specify the color of a small amount of text within a document, you can use RGB values within the <FONT> extension tag as follows:

<FONT COLOR="#RRGGBB"></FONT>*

▼ FIGURE 11-31: *Document with background and text color specified*

```
<HTML>
<BODY BGCOLOR="#000000" TEXT="#FFFFFF">
<H1>Preamble</H1>
We, the people of the United States, in order to form a more perfect
Union, establish justice, insure domestic tranquility, provide for the
common defense, promote the general welfare, and secure the bless-
ings of liberty to ourselves and our posterity, do ordain and establish
this Constitution for the United States of America.
</BODY>
</HTML>
```

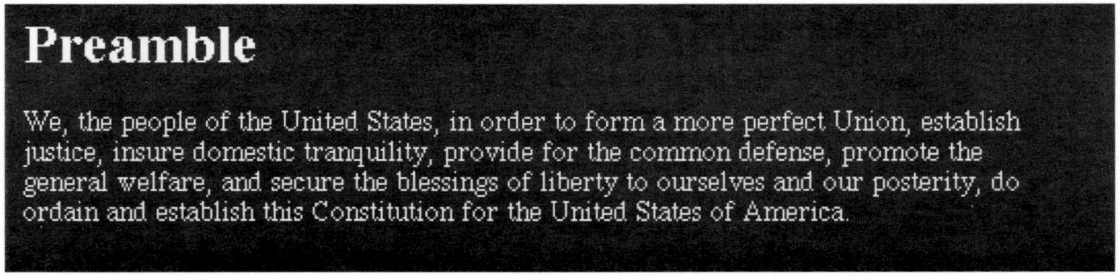

Preamble

We, the people of the United States, in order to form a more perfect Union, establish justice, insure domestic tranquility, provide for the common defense, promote the general welfare, and secure the blessings of liberty to ourselves and our posterity, do ordain and establish this Constitution for the United States of America.

Plenty of tags didn't find their way into this book. They were either too esoteric, or they control behind-the-scenes functions such as indexing and don't really contribute to the visual design of the page.

You may decide that you need to learn HTML inside and out to serve your clients well, or maybe you're just curious, or maybe you have absolutely nothing better to do. I recommend starting with some of the HTML resources and tutorials available online. People on the Web seem to love publishing information about the Web, so there is a tremendous amount of free advice available, including the following sites:

NCSA's Beginner's Guide to HTML

http://www.ncsa.uiuc.edu:80/demoweb/html-primer.html

(this document's been around a long time, but it is still very clear and helpful)

W3C (World Wide Web Consortium)

http://www.w3.org

(everything you'd ever want to know from the folks who started it all)

Netscape Home Page

http://home.netscape.com/assist/

(for all the info on the latest extensions to HTML)

Yale Web Style Manual:

http://info.med.yale.edu/caim/StyleManual_Top.HTML

Even with all these wonderful resources at my fingertips, I find it's still useful to have a thorough HTML reference book handy with complete information on all the tags and their functions. There is a dizzying variety of books available. I can certainly recommend *HTML: The Definitive Guide* by Chuck Musciano and Bill Kennedy, published by O'Reilly & Associates, which has been a terrific reference for me while writing this book.

In addition, you might want to check out *The World Wide Web Handbook: An HTML Guide for Users, Authors and Publishers*, by Peter Flynn (published by International Thomson Computer Press) which is recommended by our resident Web guru, Norm Walsh.

But of course, there's no better way to learn this stuff than to fire up a text file and try it out for yourself.

twelve   more web tricks

N THIS CHAPTER, I'd like to give you an introduction to some of the fancier things you can do with Web page design. Unfortunately, the intricacies of making these features work is beyond the scope of this book, since it has more to do with complicated programming and HTML markup than designing, but I'd be remiss in not at least showing you some of the useful tools and cool tricks that are available. Not surprisingly, they don't all work with all browsers.

I consider these elements to be part of my Web page "bag of tricks." I work with a great technical team, and as the designer, I can specify "put that element in this place," and they'll do the behind-the-scenes work. Even though some Web page designers can escape doing the actual markup and programming, it's important to keep an ear to the ground to know what features are available and how to make the most of them.

Once you get involved with Web culture, you're sure to hear buzzwords such as "Java" and "VRML." In the second part of this chapter, I'll introduce you to some of these emerging technologies and explain why they are important to the development of the Web.

■ FILL-OUT FORMS

One of the unique features of the online medium is it enables readers to provide instant feedback and information to the Web page creator, whether it's a big publisher, a retail site, or a bunch of friends sharing information about their Fantasy Baseball League.

fill-out forms

■ FOR MORE INFORMATION...

on creating forms, try out the following
step-by-step tutorials:

from Carlos A. Pero:

*http://robot0.ge.uiuc.edu/~carlosp/
cs317/cft.html*

from Web Communications:

*http://www.webcom.com/~webcom/
html/tutor/forms/*

This information can be entered through a set of input devices, such as buttons and text entry fields, collectively known as forms. Forms are part of the HTML 2.0 standard and are supported by virtually all browsers. To be functional, however, they require a program on the server.

The way forms work is that when the user fills out a form and submits his or her input, the browser sends that input to the server along with the name of a program that is specially designed to process the information. The Web server runs the program and returns its output to the browser using a special component of the server called the *Common Gateway Interface,* or CGI. The programs used to process forms are commonly known as CGI programs or CGI scripts. CGI scripts are also sometimes the key to making imagemaps functional as well, as we saw in Chapter 10, *Creating imagemaps.*

Fortunately, Web page authoring tools such as PageMill and NaviPress are beginning to provide excellent interfaces to adding forms to pages. You choose the form element you want, drag it onto the page, and the application takes care of the rest.

The following is a sampling of some of the input devices that can be used on forms (Figure 12-1):

Text entry fields

A simple text entry field allows the user to type in a single word or line of text. You can set the size of the entry box; however, unless you specify otherwise, users can enter more characters than will fit in the box (it will just scroll to the left in the field). If you want users to be able to write many lines of text, you can provide a scrolling text entry area as wide and deep as you like. A text field can also be made a "password" field, in which case asterisks will appear in place of characters on the screen.

Buttons

Checkboxes are good for yes/no, on/off types of input. Users can check off any number of checkboxes. This is not the case for radio buttons, which allow only one option to be selected from the group. "Reset" and "Submit" buttons are displayed as rectangular buttons. The reset button will clear any information entered into the form so far, and the submit button will send the information to the server. You can specify the wording in each of these buttons.

FIGURE 12-1 ▶
Form elements

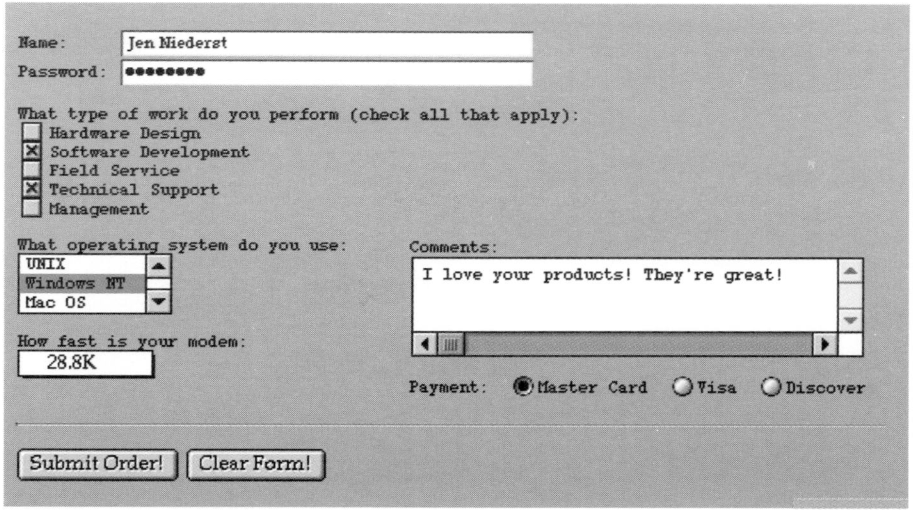

```
Name:        Jen Niederst
Password:    ●●●●●●●●

What type of work do you perform (check all that apply):
  ☐ Hardware Design
  ☒ Software Development
  ☐ Field Service
  ☒ Technical Support
  ☐ Management

What operating system do you use:        Comments:
  UNIX        ▲                           I love your products! They're great!  ▲
  Windows NT                                                                    
  Mac OS      ▼                           ◄ |||                               ► 

How fast is your modem:
  28.8K                                   Payment:  ● Master Card  ○ Visa  ○ Discover


  [ Submit Order! ]  [ Clear Form! ]
```

Menus

There are two types of menus: pull-down and scrolling. With a pull-down menu, the user can select only one of the options. Scrolling lists allow for a longer list of selections, and you can also set it so that users can select more than one option. I have recently seen both kinds of menus used as funky methods for text display on more artistically designed Web sites, such as Word *(http://www.word.com)*...yet another example of stretching HTML beyond its intended limits.

http://www.datasmith.com

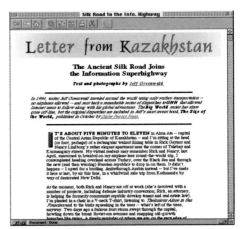

Meckler Media's Web Week Online:
http://www.webweek.com

GNN: http://gnn.com

▲ FIGURE 12-2: *Some uses of table tags*

■ FOR MORE INFORMATION...

on how to implement Netscape's tables,
see:

*http://www.netscape.com/assist/net_sites/
tables.html*

■ TABLES

Table tags can be used to create traditional charts for displaying data, such as dense scientific or business information. However, one of the real advantages to the table tags is that they are useful for creating more dynamic and even print-like page layouts (Figure 12-2). You can use table tags to create two narrow columns of text on a page or to shorten the line length of the main text column in the browser window. I'm sure this wasn't the intent of the programmers who developed the table specifications, but it's another example of designers coming up with innovative (albeit technically incorrect) uses for a limited set of tools.

However, you should be forewarned that heavy reliance on table tags to format your page could cause it to collapse into a sea of gobbledy-gook on a browser that doesn't support these tags.

The ability to display information in rows and tables has always been top on the wish-list of Web developers and designers. Nonetheless, as of this printing, it remains one of those sticky points in the standards approval process. Tags for creating tables

■ FOR MORE INFORMATION...

on how to implement frames, see
Netscape's specifications at:

*http://home.netscape.com/comprod/
   products/navigator/version_2.0/index.html*

or this guide put together by Charlton D.
Rose:

*http://pel.cs.byu.edu/~sharky/frames/
   menu.htm*

are part of the mired-down HTML 3.0 standard, still under debate. Once again, the folks at Netscape, hearing the loud chorus of demand and seeing the snail's pace of the "official" process, decided not to wait and forged ahead with their own system for creating tables on the Web.

Many browsers are rushing to support the Netscape-developed table tags, which are based on the HTML 3.0 specs, but have the usual Netscape-like embellishments. Other browsers support the straight HTML 3.0 table specifications. Still others are sticking with HTML 2.0 and don't support tables at all. Like any other non-standard feature, using table tags intensively is a little bit risky. It's best to do some testing to see whether your pages just look a little clunky or completely fall apart when they hit a non-Netscape browser.

■ FRAMES

The latest cool trick brought to us by those folks at Netscape is the "frames" capability, which works only on the Netscape Navigator browser, version 2.0. With frames, you can actually divide the traditional browser window into smaller windows, or frames, each with its own scrolling or non-scrolling capability (Figure 12-3). You can also have a link in one frame/window open the document it's pointing to in one of the other windows.

Frames create possibilities for more sophisticated interface design since you now have the ability to keep your table of contents or list of links in constant view while the reader is browsing through various documents in a separate frame.

One of the neatest things about this feature is that although the frames only display correctly in Netscape, with a little careful planning, you can use the <NOFRAMES> tag to make the same document functional on any browser. Other browsers will display information that's between the <NOFRAMES> tags and will ignore the framed information (Figure 12-4). With a little maneuvering, at least framed documents won't break other browsers attempting to display them.

FIGURE 12-3 ▶

An example of a document formatted with
Netscape frames

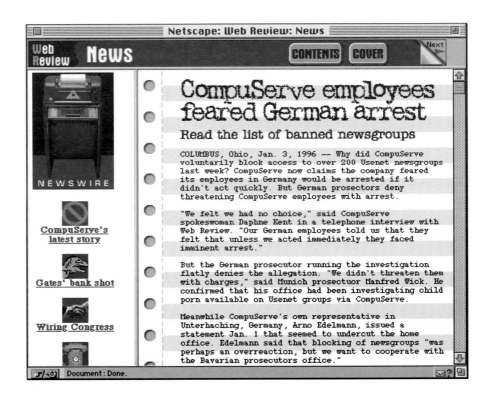

FIGURE 12-4 ▶

Careful use of <NOFRAMES> tag can allow a framed document to be functional on a non-Netscape browser.

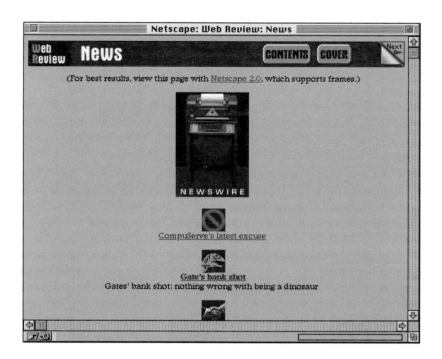

■ FOR YOUR INFORMATION

on dynamic documents, see Netscape's reference information at:

*http://home.netscape.com/assist/net_sites/
   dynamic_docs.html*

■ FOR EXAMPLES...

of server-push animation (it's nearly impossible to demonstrate in print), point your browser at:

Word (creative writing e-zine)

http://www.word.com/

Suck (a daily rant that's getting lots of attention)

http://www.suck.com/

■ DYNAMIC DOCUMENTS

By "dynamic documents," we mean Web pages that do things without the user telling them to, such as loading a new document in the window automatically, not as the result of the user clicking on a link. This sounds a little dry, but it actually has some cool uses. The most popular application is to create simple animation effects, but it can also be used to constantly update changing information (sports scores and stock information are the clichéd examples) as long as the page is displayed.

You have two main ways to make documents dynamic, both requiring a certain level of fancy tagging or CGI programming that I would generally leave up to someone more qualified than myself. These two methods are known as "client-pull" and "server-push." The difference, as the names imply, is where the commands to display new information are generated.

In client-pull, the document contains instructions to load a new document (or to reload/"refresh" the same one) after a certain interval of time. The instruction causes the browser to initiate a new connection to the server to display this new document.

With server-push, the connection is held open for an indefinite amount of time and the server essentially force-feeds the browser new information according to instructions stored on the server. Server-push is done with CGI programming.

The most popular use of server-push is to create a simple animation effect. The server simply sends out a series of GIF files as fast as it can to the browser (Figure 12-5). With a fast Net connection and good programming, the sequence of images is perceived as a little movie. The HTML file can be set up so that browsers that don't support the server-push will just display a single GIF image.

FIGURE 12-5 ▶
*One type of animation effect is created
by loading a series of inline GIF files
in rapid succession using server-push.*

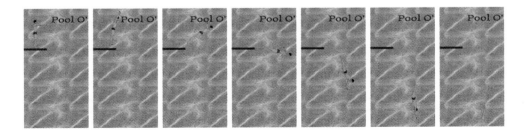

■ FOR MORE INFORMATION...

on the "flip trick," see Netscape's explanation at:

http://home.netscape.com/assist/net_sites/ impact_docs/index.html

■ THE FLIP TRICK

Netscape has developed another tricky extension, "LOWSRC," which also causes the automatic loading of an image without user input. With this extension, you can tell the browser to load a version of an inline graphic with a smaller file size and then immediately replace it with the full-color, final version. In most cases, designers use a black and white bitmapped version of the graphic as the initial image, since it will condense into a much smaller file than its full-color counterpart, yet it still contains enough image information to give some hint of the final graphic to come.

The idea is that the first graphic will load quickly, but give the user something to look at while the page and the final graphic are loading (Figure 12-6). For this reason, LOWSRC can be an alternative to interlaced GIFs (described in Chapter 9).

LOWSRC is an attribute added within the image tag. A complete tag might look like this:

```
<IMG SRC="final.gif" LOWSRC="smaller.gif">
```

FIGURE 12-6 ▶
Meckler Media's Web page uses LOWSRC to load a fast-downloading black and white image, then immediately replace it with the full-color image (http://www.mecklermedia.com/)

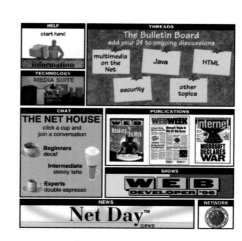

A browser that doesn't support LOWSRC will ignore it and just display the final graphic in the regular fashion. On Netscape, the graphic specified under LOWSRC ("smaller.gif") will display first, then after the remaining text and images on the page have been loaded, Netscape goes back and loads the final graphic.

■ EMERGING TECHNOLOGIES TO WATCH

When you enter the Web arena, you'll find that things are whizzing by pretty fast, and a whole slew of unfamiliar words and acronyms are bandied about regularly. It's easy to feel like you've been left behind. The following are some brief introductions to terms and technologies that you might want to be familiar with.

Shockwave

Shockwave is a new technology from Macromedia that weds multimedia documents with the Web. More specifically, the Shockwave plug-in enables the browser (currently Netscape's and NaviSoft's) to display interactive/multimedia documents (created in Director) right in the browser window. Suddenly, the elements on the browser window can really *move* and respond when you click on them. It's an exciting sight to behold.

I was thrilled the first time I saw actual animation and responsive buttons right on the page after growing so accustomed to the Web in its current blocky and static state. This is likely just a hint of things to come for online media, once the great minds get around to improving the bandwidth issue, which currently makes the transmission of really large sound and video files not worth the effort.

"Shocking" movies for the Web is as simple as taking a Macromedia Director movie file and drag-and-dropping it onto the Afterburner application (available free from Macromedia). This process creates what is called a "burned" movie file (or .dcr) which is readable by the Shockwave plug-in. As with other special Web effects, Shockwave files require some special configuring of the server, so you'll need the help of your system administrator.

The user can access the document with a URL or via a link on a page. Normally, director files will launch a player application to present the document, but with the

■ FOR MORE INFORMATION...

on Shockwave, see Macromedia's Web site at:

http://www.macromedia.com/

■ **FOR MORE INFORMATION...**

on RealAudio, see Progressive's Web page:

http://www.realaudio.com/

Shockwave plug-in, the player is built right into Netscape, so the multimedia presentation happens right in the browser window.

RealAudio

RealAudio is another technology that has drastically changed (and improved) the Web experience. Previously, to download a sound file, you had to wait for the *entire* sound file to download and then play it in the appropriate audio file player. The download times were often just not worth it, running as long as 30 minutes for a 3 minute sound clip.

With the RealAudio sound file format, the file starts playing instantly, while it is still downloading (a technique called "streaming"). You can even provide an index on the Web page to long RealAudio files, such as interviews, that provide shortcut links into the middle of the file. It is optimized to work even on a 14.4 modem, and each new release offers better sound quality. Of course, users will need the RealAudio player to play the file, but this seems like just another external tool that will be gobbled up and made a part of the fuller-functioned browsers in a matter of time.

Before you decide that you want your site to contain lots of RealAudio files, you should know that there are many pieces to the puzzle. First, you need software for translating a sound file into the RealAudio format. Second, and perhaps most importantly, the files require special RealAudio server software to make them work. You should first ask your server administrator whether using RealAudio is an option for you.

Adobe Acrobat and PDF files

Although Adobe isn't the only company developing technology for creating portable, electronic documents, it does seem to be the most aggressive in marketing their Acrobat "PDF" (Portable Document Format) as the Internet standard.

Acrobat provides a way to compactly store not just the text of a document, but all of the layout and font information, so the end-user can view the document as it was designed (a feat beyond the capacity of the Web, as we've learned). All of this information is bundled together in a PDF file. The user must have an Acrobat player to view the file, but within the viewer, the user can zoom in to see smaller details of the file, copy portions of text, and print the document with font information intact.

■ **FOR MORE INFORMATION...**

on Adobe Acrobat, see:

http://www.adobe.com/Acrobat/Acrobat.html

■ FOR MORE INFORMATION...

on VRML, look at Yahoo
(http://www.yahoo.com) under Computers
and Internet/World Wide Web/Virtual Reality Modeling Language, or look at these
sites:

VRML Forum (good general information by
VRML's creators):

http://vrml.wired.com/

List of cool VRML sites:

http://www.paperinc.com/wrls.html

Adobe has worked out a deal with Netscape (and I anticipate other browsers are soon to follow) that will embed the Acrobat viewer right into their browser. With this plug-in, the PDF file displays right in the browser window without launching an external viewer.

Electronic documents are an effective way to distribute certain types of information over the Net, and publishers of this information love the control over presentation that they lose in HTML. Even with the ability to display right in the browser window, I don't see PDF replacing HTML as the primary method for sending pages over the lines, but it is a useful tool in some circumstances.

VRML

VRML, which stands for "Virtual Reality Modeling Language," is a technology developed by Silicon Graphics and a host of other contributors for describing three-dimensional spaces. What makes VRML different from other 3-D computer-generated worlds is that it is specially formatted to be distributed over the Web and can even contain hyperlinks within the space. These hyperlinks can link to other Web pages or to other VRML spaces. To view VRML files, you need a special VRML browser or a plug-in to Netscape.

The technology is in its infancy, but proponents envision rich VRML spaces which serve as interfaces to complex databases, *à la* Gibson's *Neuromancer*. We aren't at that point yet; however, already you can take a virtual tour of San Francisco's "Soma" district (Figure 12-7), which houses a glut of multi-media companies. I've also used a simple VRML world as an interface to a multi-part story, in which you clicked on the building, and it linked to an HTML story about that building. VRML's practical uses are still being debated and developed. Nevertheless, it's one of those Internet buzzwords and a technology to be aware of.

Java

And speaking of technologies to be aware of, perhaps the grand-daddy of them all is Java—developed by Sun—which is expected to have a big impact on the Web. Java is a streamlined programming language that can be used to create applications that are platform-independent. This format makes it ideal for distribution over the Internet,

which is made up of a dizzying variety of machines and operating systems. Java only requires that the computer have an "interpreter" application to read the Java code.

Many programmers have used Java to create programs, commonly known as "applets." An applet can be a game, a working spreadsheet, or the most popular applet-*du-jour*, animation. This is only the beginning; the sky's the limit on the functions Java applets can perform.

The key to Java is that the applets are downloaded from the server upon request, and all the functions take place on the client side. Thus, Java is a preferable tool for creating animation because with Java the server doesn't continuously feed new images to the browser, but downloads an entire program for the browser to run locally. With client-pull and server-push, the speed at which your document is updated is at the mercy of the speed of the network. On a slow day, animation might crawl. With Java, since the program is downloaded to the user's machine, the network is out of the picture, and documents can zip along.

Sun's browser HotJava (written in the Java language) actually incorporates each applet it encounters, so you have the possibility of browsers that get better as you use them.

Recently, Netscape began supporting Java applets in version 2.0 of its Navigator browser, thus bringing Java technology to the masses. To learn more about Java, see *Java in a Nutshell* and *Exploring Java*, both published by O'Reilly & Associates.

■ FOR MORE INFORMATION...

on the Java programming language and its splash on the Web, see Sun Microsystem's page:

http://java.sun.com/

thirteen **from web page to web site**

HANCES ARE, YOU WON'T BE asked to create a single Web page for a client. Even if you are just creating a home page for yourself or your family, it makes sense to take advantage of the Web's linking ability and break up your information logically over many connected Web pages (a page for Greg, a page for Marcia, a page for Cindy, etc.).

This book has focused on the nuts and bolts of assembling the text and graphics that make up a Web page. We've also taken a look at how two Web pages get linked together (Chapter 4). But an effective Web site is more than a tangle of connected pages. It requires some planning and sensitivity to the user on the part of the designer.

All design shapes a user's experience. Graphic designers can affect how information is perceived on a page and in what order. An architect designs not just the building, but the visitor's experience walking through it. Similarly, a Web site designer needs to consider the user's experience of "moving through" the pages of a Web site, as though through rooms in a building.

On the Web, the experience-shaping aspect of design is perhaps even more pronounced since it is interactive and a little fragmented by nature. Pages of a book are stitched together, but pages on a Web site can be accessed practically randomly, which can lead to confusion.

Although I can't treat the vast topic of interface design thoroughly, in this chapter I'll share some of my own experiences in site-planning to give you a flavor of what you may encounter when creating a multi-page Web site.

■ CONCEPTUALIZING

Just as you would for any other design project, start your Web site design by asking some big questions, such as:

What is the function of this site?

Web surfers generally fall into two categories: those on a mission to find information or get something done, and those who are there for the ride. Is your site primarily about distributing information or providing entertainment? Informational or service-oriented sites should provide the goods quickly and clearly without a lot of bandwidth-gobbling production effects. Sites that aim to create an experience or a place to play may get away with more graphics and cool effects since that's usually part of what their audience wants.

Often you'll find that your site falls somewhere in between. In that case, the trick is to strike a comfortable balance between presentation and performance.

Would a metaphor help?

Sometimes, it is helpful to base your site on another more familiar model to give users a headstart on understanding how elements fit together and how the site works.

For instance, when I designed the online magazine *Web Review,** I used visual cues that referred to a print magazine. Instead of a home page, *Web Review* has a cover, and there are even references to paper with ripped or folded-back edges. For this site, it made sense to hold on to some notion of the "page."

Other sites use towns, stores, or radio as their metaphors. They can be an effective approach, but be forewarned that metaphors sometimes fall apart since not every aspect of a Web site has an exact real-world equivalent.

Will the site be interactive?

One aspect of the Web that makes it different from any other medium is its ability to accept instant feedback from the reader. For this reason, when thinking about the site, you need to consider not just how much information it will provide, but also how

*You can view *Web Review* at *http://www.webreview.com/*. Note that in response to user feedback, we are in a constant state of re-design and experimentation. The site may look quite different than it does in the examples in this chapter, which were current as of this writing.

much and what type of information you'd like to receive. Many sites on the Web strongly encourage reader involvement by making feedback opportunities an integral part of their interface. On others, feedback is limited to a form for ordering a product.

■ ORGANIZING AND PLANNING

Inventory

Since I'm a nearly compulsive list-maker, I usually start by doing an inventory of *everything* I'd like the site to include. At first, I don't worry too much about how the elements are organized and what links to what; it's just a good exercise to get everything jotted down on a pad of paper to see what you have.

Logical groupings usually become apparent just by seeing all of the elements listed in one place. You can then begin to think about how each group of information is related to another, and whether the groups need to be reached in any particular order.

Organizational diagram

Next, you need to organize the information on your site. When I'm ready for this stage of design, I find that drawing a diagram of the site is the best way to get a handle on the site as a whole. I usually add arrows representing the links that are available on each page. That way, I can check for navigational dead-ends, such as pages that you can get to but don't offer any way out (except for hitting the browser's "back" button a dozen times).

Hierarchical structure

Most Web sites are organized hierarchically, starting with a top page that offers several choices and then successive layers of choices branching out below each, so that a "tree" is formed (Figure 13-1).

Hierarchical organization is a tried-and-true method, and, if done well, it offers the user clear, step-by-step access to material on the site. If you choose this structure, there are a few guidelines you should follow.

FIGURE 13-1 ▶

Diagram of site with a hierarchical organization

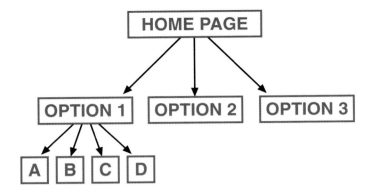

First, make sure that important information doesn't get buried down too deeply. With each required click, you run the risk of losing a few readers who may only have time to skim through the top layers of a site.

Also, make sure that the branches of the hierarchy "tree" are balanced. For example, avoid making one branch fifteen levels deep when all the others have only two or three levels of information.

Linear arrangement

Although tree-style structure is the most popular and multi-purpose, it is by no means your only option, and may not be the best suited for your type of information. You may also consider organizing your site (or part of it) linearly, particularly if you are serving narrative information or if it is important that pages be viewed in a particular order.

Figure 13-2 is a diagram I did for a particular multi-part story written for *Web Review*. As you can see from the diagram, the reader starts with the first Web page, and moves in one direction through the story (wiggly lines represent links to the Net, outside of *Web Review*). From my original diagram, I found that there was a dead end when the reader got to the last document in the chain linked under the third page, so I made sure to provide an "escape hatch" by creating a link to the next page of the story. Otherwise, the reader's only choice would have been to hit the "back" button on the

browser repeatedly to be able to continue on with the main story. That's a situation
you don't want to inflict on your readers, so make sure it's easy to keep moving.

In fact, the entire *Web Review* magazine is organized linearly, one story following
another, consistent with the magazine metaphor I established in the beginning. The
table of contents provides a map of what the issue contains as well as links directly to
each story.

Other structures

Obviously, there are as many possible structures as there are Web sites. Experiment
with alternative structures. I recommend working this phase out on paper before com-
mitting it to HTML (although you'll need to do some user testing later to be sure it's
effective). The important thing is to create an organizational plan that is appropriate,
and then be sure that it's clear to the user. Remember to put yourself in the user's place
throughout the process.

■ ORIENTATIONAL AND NAVIGATIONAL AIDS

The larger and more complicated your site, the greater the chance for users to get
completely lost or to miss out on a large chunk of the value you're offering. For this

reason, provide clear and consistent clues that first tell them where they are and then provide options for where to go next.

In *Web Review,* I designed the following navigational bar ("navbar" for short) to provide this functionality. Let's take a look at its different parts:

1   2   3

Clear labeling

Remember that a user can enter your site from any point if they have the right URL. There's no guarantee that they will have the benefit of the home page to tell them what's up, so it's important that every page contain some label that says where they've arrived.

In the navbar, I've made sure that "Web Review" is clearly stamped on every story in the magazine (1). That way, if someone is directed to a particular page, he or she will know where they are.

In addition, if your site has different sections or levels, it is a good idea to orient the reader within the site's structure. In the example above, it is clear that you are in *Web Review,* in the Technology section (2). In the original GNN, I used a row of icons that accumulated as you dug deeper into GNN's many levels. You could tell by the row of icons that you were in the Notes section, within the Travel Section, within GNN (the icons also served as links to the higher levels).

Navigational tools

By providing graphical buttons or text links, you can make it easier for users to move throughout the site. I usually ask myself two questions in deciding exactly what buttons and how many to add to each page I design. For the first question, I put myself in the shoes of the user: Where might that person want to go next? For the second question, I play the role of the publisher or Web site creator: Where do *I* want that person to go next? For complicated sites, providing access to every page of the site from every other page on the site can result in an overwhelming maze. By limiting choices, you can hope to shape the user's experience of your site.

■ INTERFACE DESIGN TIP

Long lists of choices can be overwhelming and do not encourage browsing. The magic number in interface design is seven—that is, the human brain tends to short-circuit when faced with more than seven options at a shot. If it's necessary to have a large number of items available on a page, find a way to break them into a few major groups.

■ NAVIGATIONAL TIP

If you have a long list of items that each link to separate, single pages, it's nice to provide a navigational button or text link that allows the reader to get directly to the next page on the list without having to go back to the main list page each time. It makes for a more pleasant browsing experience, and may result in the reader visiting more of your pages.

In my *Web Review* navbar, I have provided only three navigational buttons (3). I chose the cover because it is the main point of entry to the publication. I figured that if a reader started there, even though it isn't as thorough as the contents page, that person might want to go back there to follow an interesting link he or she spotted when first entering. For me, nothing is more annoying than entering a site at a certain point and then never being able to find that page again from within the site.

I provided a prominent link to the contents page because it contains a complete listing of the stories and features offered in that issue. From that page, you can link directly to any of the stories. But once in a story, I want to encourage the reader to stay in the magazine, so I added an easy and tempting link directly to the next story. Using the "next" button, you can flip through the stories in *Web Review* quickly, as though flipping the pages of a printed magazine.

Display navigational tools consistently

Providing navigational options is not enough if they aren't predictable or dependable. It's very important that navigational options be consistent throughout the site, both in availability as well as in appearance.

Pages that are alike should have the same navigational options. If I could get back to the home page directly from one second-level page, I'd expect to be able to get back there from all the others as well. Third-level pages might have a different set of options, but that set of options needs to be consistent amongst all other third-level pages, and so on.

Furthermore, I think it helps usability to present the options in the same fashion every time they're presented. If your home page button appears in blue at the top right hand corner of the page, don't put it at the bottom in red on another page. If you are offering a whole list of options, such as in a toolbar, keep the selections in the same order on each page, so users don't have to spend time hunting around for the option they just used a minute ago. In *Web Review*, I use the same navbar on the top of every story (with the appropriate section title displayed, of course).

All of this may seem obvious, but you'd be surprised at all the professional Web sites that are nearly impossible to get around; or once you get in, you can never get back to the same page again. If you keep yourself in the user's point of view and do your planning early, you may be able to nip these problems in the bud.

■ THE FINAL WORD: TEST

I want to stress one more time the benefit of testing. You may regularly test your graphics and HTML files under different conditions to see what may happen to them, but the real test of a site's success can only come from feedback from real human beings.

Tools and structures that seem perfectly obvious to you may perplex others. There are so many ways to slice it, it sometimes requires a few tries to work out the bugs. A user-testing session is a valuable stage in this process.

I run two types of tests. One is a browsing free-for-all, where I just point users at the site and let them roam, noting where they choose to go first and asking them why they made the choices they did. In the other, I give them a mission to accomplish, such as "find the article on ISDN lines," then see how long it takes them to find it. If they are completely stumped or meander around too long, then perhaps I haven't provided strong enough clues to how the site is organized, or perhaps the way I've named things isn't clear.

The important thing is to be very open to user feedback during the testing phase. Sometimes it is hard to step out of the project enough to get a clear, objective perspective. As much as you may love your concepts and graphics, the purpose is defeated if your audience can't use them to get to the information they need.

index

◼ ABOUT THE AUTHORS

JENNIFER NIEDERST is the Creative Director of Songline Studios, publishers of innovative online products. She began designing documents for the World Wide Web in mid-1993 as the original designer of the identity, interface, and graphics for Global Network Navigator (GNN), published by O'Reilly & Associates, Inc.

Prior to her life online, Jennifer worked as a book designer for O'Reilly & Associates, Inc., and Little, Brown & Company. She has also worked as a freelance graphic designer. She attended the University of Notre Dame where she received a BFA in design and photography and a BA in art history.

EDIE FREEDMAN has been the Creative Director of O'Reilly and Associates, Inc. for the past 6 years. Her design work for O'Reilly includes book covers, packaging, company identity, and Web design. She is also president of Freedman Kennedy Design, Inc., a small graphic design firm serving corporate clients in the Boston area.

◼ COLOPHON

PATRICK PIERCE is a sculptor, painter, and poet who lives and works in the Boston area. The cover image is derived from a painted assemblage entitled "New Wilderness." For more information on Patrick Pierce and his work, send email to: *pierce@vmsmkt.enet.dec.com.*

Illustrations by CHRIS REILLEY.

Interior design and production by SEVENTEENTH STREET STUDIOS, Oakland.

Production tools: QuarkXpress 3.3, Adobe Photoshop 3.0, and Macromedia FreeHand 5.0, all on the Macintosh platform.

Types: Sabon (Adobe), ITC Legacy Sans (Adobe), Digitek (Fontek), Univers (Adobe).

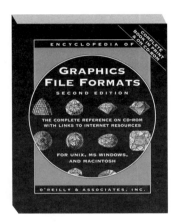

Stay in touch with O'REILLY™

Visit Our Award-Winning World Wide Web Site
http://www.ora.com/

Voted

"**Top 100 Sites on the Web**" —*PC Magazine*
"**Top 5% Web sites**" —*Point Communications*
"**3-Star site**" —*The McKinley Group*

Our web site contains a library of comprehensive product information (including book excerpts and tables of content), downloadable software, background articles, interviews with technology leaders, links to relevant sites, book cover art, and more. Add us to your Bookmarks or Hotlist!

Join Our Two Email Mailing Lists

LIST #1   NEW PRODUCT RELEASES: To receive automatically via your email box brief descriptions of all new O'Reilly products as they are released, send email to: **listproc@online.ora.com** and put the following information in the first line of your message (NOT in the *Subject:* field, which is ignored): **subscribe ora-news "Your Name" of "Your Organization"** (for example: **subscribe ora-news Kris Webber of Fine Enterprises**)

LIST #2   O'REILLY EVENTS: If you'd also like us to send information about trade show events, special promotions, and other O'Reilly events, send email to: **listproc@online.ora.com** and put the following information in the first line of your message (NOT in the *Subject:* field, which is ignored): **subscribe ora-events "Your Name" of "Your Organization"**

Visit Our Gopher Site

- Connect your gopher to **gopher.ora.com**, or
- Point your web browser to **gopher://gopher.ora.com/**, or
- telnet to **gopher.ora.com** (login: **gopher**)

Get example files from our books via FTP

There are two ways to access an archive of example files from our books:

REGULAR FTP — ftp to: **ftp.ora.com** (login: anonymous—use your email address as the password) or point your web browser to: **ftp://ftp.ora.com/**

FTPMAIL — Send an email message to: **ftpmail@online.ora.com** (write help in the message body)

Contact Us Via Email

order@ora.com — To place a book or software order on-line. Good for North American and International customers.

subscriptions@ora.com — To place an order for any of our newsletters or periodicals.

software@ora.com — General questions and product information about our software.
  - Check out O'Reilly Software Online at http://software.ora.com for software and technical support information.
  - Registered O'Reilly software users send your questions to website-support@ora.com

books@ora.com — General questions about any of our books.

cs@ora.com — For answers to problems regarding your order or our product.

booktech@ora.com — For book content technical questions or corrections.

proposals@ora.com — To submit new book or software proposals to our editors and product managers.

international@ora.com — Information about our international distributors or translation queries
  - Check out http://www.ora.com/www/order/country.html for a list of our distributors outside of North America.

O'REILLY™

101 Morris Street, Sebastopol, CA 95472 USA
707-829-0515 or 800-998-9938 (6 A.M. to 5 P.M. PST); FAX 707-829-0104

TO ORDER: **800-889-8969** (CREDIT CARD ORDERS ONLY); **order@ora.com**
Our products are available at a bookstore or software store near you.

International Distributors

Customers outside North America can now order O'Reilly & Associates books through the following distributors. They offer our international customers faster order processing, more bookstores, increased representation at tradeshows worldwide, and the high-quality, responsive service our customers have come to expect.

EUROPE, MIDDLE EAST AND AFRICA
(except Germany, Switzerland, and Austria)

INQUIRIES
International Thomson Publishing Europe
Berkshire House
168-173 High Holborn
London WC1V 7AA, United Kingdom
Telephone: 44-71-497-1422
Fax: 44-71-497-1426
Email: **itpint@itps.co.uk**

ORDERS
International Thomson Publishing Services, Ltd.
Cheriton House, North Way
Andover, Hampshire SP10 5BE,
United Kingdom
Telephone: 44-264-342-832 (UK orders)
Telephone: 44-264-342-806 (outside UK)
Fax: 44-264-364418 (UK orders)
Fax: 44-264-342761 (outside UK)

GERMANY, SWITZERLAND, AND AUSTRIA

International Thomson Publishing GmbH
O'Reilly-International Thomson Verlag
Königswinterer Straße 418
53227 Bonn, Germany
Telephone: 49-228-97024 0
Fax: 49-228-441342
Email: **anfragen@ora.de**

AUSTRALIA
WoodsLane Pty. Ltd.
7/5 Vuko Place, Warriewood NSW 2102
P.O. Box 935, Mona Vale NSW 2103
Australia
Telephone: 61-2-9970-5111
Fax: 61-2-9970-5002
Email: **woods@tmx.mhs.oz.au**

NEW ZEALAND
WoodsLane New Zealand Ltd.
21 Cooks Street (P.O. Box 575)
Wanganui, New Zealand
Telephone: 64-6-347-6543
Fax: 64-6-345-4840
Email: **info@woodslane.com.au**

THE AMERICAS
O'Reilly & Associates, Inc.
101 Morris Street
Sebastopol, CA 95472 U.S.A.
Telephone: 707-829-0515
Telephone: 800-998-9938 (U.S. & Canada)
Fax: 707-829-0104
Email: **order@ora.com**

ASIA *(except Japan and India)*
INQUIRIES
International Thomson Publishing Asia
60 Albert St. #15-01
Albert Complex
Singapore 189969
Telephone: 65-272-6496
Fax: 65-336-6411

ORDERS
Telephone: 65-336-6411
Fax: 65-334-1617

JAPAN
O'Reilly Japan, Inc.
Kiyoshige Building 2F
12-Bancho, Sanei-cho
Shinjuku-ku
Tokyo 160 Japan
Telephone: 81 3 3356 55227
Fax: 81 3 3356 5261
Email: **kenji@ora.com**

INDIA
Computer Bookshop (India) PVT. LTD.
190 Dr. D.N. Road, Fort
Bombay 400 001
India
Telephone: 91-22-207-0989
Fax: 91-22-262-3551
Email: **cbsbom@giasbm01.vsnl.net.in**